JOHNNY WINTER

A Step-by-Step Breakdown of his
Guitar Styles and Techniques

by Dave Rubin

Cover photo by Neil Zlozower

ISBN 978-1-4234-1641-8

HAL•LEONARD® CORPORATION

7777 W. BLUEMOUND RD. P.O. BOX 13819 MILWAUKEE, WI 53213

Visit Hal Leonard Online at
www.halleonard.com

FOREWORD

It is an honor to present Johnny Winter and his best music. No one is more deserving. His passion for the blues and the rock 'n' roll that it bore is unsurpassed and "still alive and well." Brought up on and inspired by such legendary blues guitarists as T-Bone Walker, Muddy Waters, and B.B. King, he has earned his place in the pantheon of the greats. However, even as Gibson is issuing a signature Johnny Winter Firebird, he is far from resting on his laurels, continuing to play, tour, and record while showing no signs of slowing down. Grab a signature Firebird for the correct Johnny Winter vibe if you can, but what is more important is to bring the same fire, desire, and love to learning his music as he did when creating it.

DEDICATION AND ACKNOWLEDGMENTS

This book is dedicated to Nick Koukotas, a great friend, guitarist, and the biggest Johnny Winter fan I know. I would also like to thank the following for their help and support: Paul Nelson, Sean McDevitt, Bruce Iglauer, Dick Shurman, Eric Leblanc, Zeke Shein, Ed Komara, Joe Denig, Mark Freed, and John Stix.

Dave Rubin
NYC, 2007

CONTENTS

Page	Title	CD Track
4	Johnny Winter: White Heat, White Light	
8	The Recording	
	Tuning	1
9	**Bad Luck Situation**	2–7
16	**Be Careful with a Fool**	8–11
25	**Bladie Mae**	12–15
33	**Highway 61 Revisited**	16–19
38	**It Was Raining**	20–22
44	**Leland Mississippi**	23–27
49	**Mean Town Blues**	28–32
57	**Rock and Roll Hoochie Koo**	33–38
64	**Rock Me Baby**	39–44
71	**Still Alive and Well**	45–50
77	**Sweet Love and Evil Women**	51–56
87	**TV Mama**	57–62
94	Guitar Notation Legend	

JOHNNY WINTER: WHITE HEAT, WHITE LIGHT

As if to mock the very notion of whether or not a "white man can play the blues," Johnny Winter, with his nearly translucent albino skin and blindingly white hair, blasted down the doors starting in the late 1960s for everyone who loved the music. He once said, perhaps ironically, "In my own mind, I was the best white blues player around," but clearly that qualification no longer applies. The legendary Lonnie Mack and the British contingent of Eric Clapton, Peter Green, Mick Taylor, and Jimmy Page before him had shown the possibilities of rocking the blues, but no one was adequately prepared for Winter. Notes flew from his fingers like blazing blue diamonds, creating shock and awe for everyone within sight and earshot. It was the perfect culmination to the blues revival with Winter carrying the torch while throwing gasoline on the fire. He would go on to not only influence fellow Texans like Billy Gibbons and Stevie Ray Vaughan, but also the stone Chicago blues cat Bernard Allison. Most significantly, for more than forty years he has played and contributed to the musical language of the blues in ways that were only strengthened by his numerous forays into rock.

John Dawson Winter III was born in Leland, Mississippi on February 23, 1944 to John and Edwina, but was raised in Beaumont, Texas. The senior Winter, a career Army officer who sang, played saxophone and banjo, and was a fan of the big bands, encouraged Johnny and his younger brother Edgar to pursue music. John's father had been a cotton broker in Leland and after WWII attempted to take over the business, becoming the boss at the storied Stovall Plantation, an important figure in early blues history.

Johnny was singing and playing the clarinet by five, but eventually quit clarinet when an orthodontist advised against it due to his overbite. Three years later he added the ukulele to his repertoire and then was given the baritone variety by his grandfather. By 1954 he and Edgar were appearing as a duo, singing barbershop quartet songs like "Ain't She Sweet" and "Bye Bye Blackbird," and even auditioning for the nationally broadcasted Ted Mack's Original Amateur Hour. It was about this time that Winter's father offered the opinion that there were only two people, Ukulele Ike and Arthur Godfrey, who had ever amounted to anything on the diminutive stringed instrument, and that the guitar might prove to be a better choice. The advice was heeded, especially after Winter realized that the emerging rock 'n' roll music at the time was played on the guitar. Within the year, he was learning note-for-note guitar solos off the records he bought by mowing lawns, hauling garbage, and saving his lunch money. T-Bone Walker, Howlin' Wolf, Muddy Waters, Chuck Berry, and Carl Perkins were favorites with *The Best of Muddy Waters* being an early purchase and the records of Robert Johnson inspiring him to play slide guitar. He recalls shopping regularly at a record shop owned by Keith Ferguson's father years before Ferguson became the bassist for the Fabulous Thunderbirds. Winter's first guitar was his great-grandmother's "hundred-year old classical guitar." Later, his great-grandfather bought him his first electric guitar, a Gibson ES-125, non-cutaway, with a single P-90 pickup.

There were not many white people in Beaumont in the 1950s as seriously into playing and listening to the blues as Winter. One of the few was Joey Long (nee Longoria) who was a little older, and the first white man Winter heard play the music. Like almost all electric blues guitarists from Texas, he was profoundly influenced by T-Bone Walker. Winter, on the other hand, while acknowledging his debt to the legendary electric blues pioneer, also had a strong love for Chicago blues not always shared by his fellow musicians.

When Winter would hear blues guitar idols like Otis Rush push and vibrato their strings, he would marvel at how it was done, not realizing at the time that it was as much an expression of their inner soulfulness as the lighter gauge strings they were using. For a while he accomplished the technique with a whammy bar. Ever open to whatever blues caught his fancy, it was the expert string articulation of Clapton that would eventually convince Winter around 1967 to become an acknowledged master of finger vibrato and bending.

In 1959, with Johnny on guitar and Edgar accompanying on piano, Johnny & The Jammers promptly won a local talent contest sponsored by radio station KTRM. Their prize consisted of a recording session, and they cut the single "School Day Blues" b/w "You Know I Love You," ultimately released by Dart Records. It became a regional hit, resulting in Winter being called to provide guitar on record dates supervised by local promoters and producers. As was the custom in those days, the music he was playing was what people wanted to hear—rock 'n' roll, R&B, and then soul music—not blues. All the while he was compulsively woodshedding his chops and voraciously listening to all the blues recordings he could find. A treasure trove resided at radio station KJET where DJ and bluesman Clarence Garlow of the Bon Ton show befriended him, took his requests on air, and let him hang at the station while also showing him guitar techniques. "I first saw him at Jefferson Music Company where I worked as a guitar teacher," Winter explains. "He walked in and I recognized his voice. His style was similar to T-Bone Walker. On his show he also played a lot of his own records" laughs Winter. "I was about twelve years old, and he was one of the first guitar players to use light gauge strings, and he taught me how to use an unwound third. We jammed together a few times, too, including once at my house that was great."

Winter cites Chet Atkins and Merle Travis as guitarists who really made him want to play (and his impetus for using a thumbpick). He learned the rudiments of country fingerstyle from Jefferson Music coworker Luther Naley and some jazz from Seymour Drugan, the father of Dennis Drugan (the bass player for the Jammers). He briefly attended Lamar University in Beaumont after high school, sneaking down to Louisiana on the weekends to jam in the blues clubs. There and in Texas he was often the only white person in the club, but felt welcome for the most part due to his obvious and sincere love for the music.

His perseverance and total immersion in the blues gained him access to the local scene by 1963 where he got to jam with B.B. King in a momentous occasion. The following year he took a pilgrimage to Chicago to join Dennis Drugan in the Gents where he hoped to play blues, but instead ended up once again performing the popular music of the day. While in the Windy City he met Michael Bloomfield at his club, the Fickle Pickle, for what would become a solid friendship based on mutual admiration. Winter was back in Texas a year later, however, and cut "Eternally" for the KRCO label, which leased it to Atlantic Records, scoring a regional hit that allowed him to advance to the next level— touring and opening for rock acts like Jerry Lee Lewis and the Everly Brothers. In 1967 he made a fortuitous move to Houston, a hot bed for blues in the Lone Star State, and convened a trio with bassist Tommy Shannon and drummer Uncle John "Red" Turner, who in turn encouraged Winter to concentrate on performing the blues, knowing he was mastering the style at a rapid pace. The band became a fixture at the Vulcan Gas Company ballroom, later dubbed Armadillo World Headquarters, and Winter's reputation soared on the wings of his impossibly fast, furious, and fluid solos. While in residency he got to play with Freddie King and met Muddy Waters for the first time, with whom he would form a lifelong friendship. In addition, responding to the creative rock experimentation going on in the late 1960s, he also tried his hand at the psychedelic experience musically and sartorially.

Winter's big break came in 1968 when *Rolling Stone* magazine prominently featured him in an article about the vital and burgeoning Texas blues scene. Almost overnight a bidding war erupted for his services, with New York impresario Steve Paul scurrying on down to Texas to sign the exciting new blues blood and bring him back to his Scene night club on West 46th Street and 8th Avenue, a block from Times Square. On a Friday night in December, he sat in with his old acquaintance Mike Bloomfield and his pal Al Kooper at the Fillmore East in Manhattan. After an exceedingly enthusiastic introduction by Bloomfield, Winter preceded to take over vocally and instrumentally on "It's My Own Fault." By Monday morning he had signed a much ballyhooed contract with Columbia Records, the details of which have never been revealed, and received a $168,000 advance, considered astronomical for the time.

Johnny Winter and *Second Winter* were released in 1969. The former clocked in at an impressive #24 on the charts and featured the epic and epochal slow blues burner "Be Careful with a Fool," the autobiographical "Leland Mississippi Blues," and legendary bassist/producer/songwriter Willie Dixon and harp maestro Big Walter "Shakey" Horton as guest artists. *Second Winter* contained Bob Dylan's "Highway 61 Revisited," a perennial in Winter's live sets ever since and evidence of his exquisite taste in covers. It made a respectable showing at #55. Preceding them both by some months on Imperial Records, however, was *The Progressive Blues Experiment*, originally recorded in 1967, creating some confusion among his fans as to his official debut. Whatever the chronology, that record was a collection of some of the purest and most intense blues he would ever play, including his boogie classic "Meantown Blues," and it put him squarely on the map among his fellow guitarists. It topped out at #40 and has lost none of its wrenching emotive power over the years.

Life in New York for the transplanted Texan revolved around the Scene where he regularly jammed with Jimi Hendrix—whom he calls his "favorite rock and roll guitar player"—among other rock luminaries. Both superstars claimed they were "groupies" of the other and recorded a version of Guitar Slim's the "Things I Used to Do" that appeared on the bootleg ghoulishly titled *Woke Up This Morning and Found Myself Dead*. Both also played the Woodstock Festival in August of 1969, though Winter missed the opportunity for his exceptional performance to appear in the influential movie that made superstars out of lesser acts like Ten Years After. Winter also played at Hendrix's funeral less than a year later in 1970.

Steve Paul convinced Winter that the blues revival had overdosed people on the music and that he should do more rock and add a second guitar player. He joined forces with ex-McCoy guitarist Rick Derringer for the band Johnny Winter And, a smash outfit capable of playing the real deal blues and fist-pumping rock 'n' roll. Their self-titled debut released in 1970 featured the classic "Rock and Roll Hoochie Koo" penned by Derringer and later covered by him on his first solo album. Johnny Winter And's spectacular live album from 1971 went gold (#40) and belongs in the same company as *Live at the Fillmore East* from the Allman Brothers Band. It remains Winter's top-selling album to this day. Unfortunately, years of substance abuse, including heroin, caught up with him around this time, while his band with Derringer was backing brother Edgar in the contemporary R&B band White Trash. Winter checked himself into a detox center in New Orleans and came out nine months later clean and sober. When he emerged with the great Derringer-produced *Still Alive and Well* in 1973, it rocked to #22, his top charting position, and renewed Winter's physical and musical health. The title track and a scorching version of Big Bill Broonzy's "Rock Me Baby" stood out among a set that also included the Stones' "Silver Train," personally presented by Richards and Jagger to Winter to cover first, as perhaps acknowledgement of his devastating cover of "Jumpin' Jack Flash" from *Live Johnny Winter And*.

Through to 1976 Winter was literally on top of the rock world as the top arena draw and he released a string of excellent albums that acknowledged his blues roots tangentially. *Saints and Sinners* from 1974 had the blues-rocking "Bad Luck Situation" as well as the Stones' lascivious "Stray Cat Blues," while *John Dawson Winter III* from the same year represented his move to Blue Sky Records, a subsidiary of Columbia. *Captured Live*, released two years later, boasted "Rock & Roll People," a "gift" from John Lennon to Winter. 1977, however, marked a turning point in his recording career from which he has not significantly deviated since. *Nothin' But the Blues*, followed a year later by *White, Hot and Blue*, are unvarnished, down home blues albums. The former contains "Bladie Mae," "It Was Rainin'," "Sweet Love and Evil Women," and "TV Mama" with backing from Muddy Waters and his band with guitarist "Steady Rollin'" Bob Margolin. As one of the high points of his career, Winter would receive the opportunity to return the favor to his idol when he produced and played on *Hard Again* (1977), *I'm Ready* (1978), the Grammy-winning *Muddy "Mississippi" Waters Live* (1979), and *King Bee* (1981).

After taking a substantial break from the recording studio following *Raisin' Cain* in 1980 and helping out Uncle John Turner on his *Gulf Coast Blues* album, Winter returned with a new label and a renewed sense of purpose. Signing with Alligator Records resulted in the "house-rocking" Grammy-nominated *Guitar Slinger* (1984) and *Serious Business* (1985), along with *Third Degree* (1986). The fit at Alligator was tight, with vocal and guitar performances and songs rivaling his best, early work for Columbia, and he was featured on MTV's *Guitar Greats* special. But by 1988 he had switched labels again for *The Winter of '88* on Voyager Records, for which he took a side trip back to rock, followed by the more successful, both commercially and artistically, *Let Me In* on Pointblank Records in 1991. Produced by renown blues expert, DJ, and writer Dick Shurman, who had been so instrumental in the Alligator recordings, it fairly exploded with Winter's old energy and boasted cameos by Albert Collins, Dr. John, and his boyhood friend from Texas, Dennis Drugan. The single "Illustrated Man," climbed all the way to #36, a first for Winter. Revitalized once again on the new label, he released *Hey, Where's Your Brother?* in 1992 with Edgar in tow, and featuring the single "Please Come Home for Christmas."

The 1990s saw the beginning of a slow decline in Winter's health and career, both, at least partly, the result of his management. Various collections of previously released material and other ventures, including a record with his old drummer, Uncle John Turner, kept his name in front of the public, but it took *Live in NYC '97*, once again produced by Dick Shurman, to confirm that he could still blow away any pretenders to the high-powered blues guitar throne. Recorded at the famous Bottom Line in Greenwich Village, it boogied all the way to #7 on the charts.

It was the Grammy-nominated and likewise #7 charting *I'm a Bluesman* in 2005 on Virgin/EMI (his first release of new material in eight years) that helped right Winter's career again. Produced by Dick Shurman along with Tom Hambridge, the album featured veteran harp man James Montgomery, guitarist Paul Nelson, and ex-Double Trouble keyboardist Reese Wynans. Today, Johnny Winter is still going strong, touring the world over as the international ambassador of rockin' Texas blues. Check out **www.johnnywinter.net** to stay updated on his curent projects and tour dates.

THE RECORDING

Doug Boduch: guitar
Warren Wiegratz: keyboards
Tom McGirr: bass
Scott Schroedl: drums

Recorded and produced by Jake Johnson & Bill Maynard, Paradyme Productions.

Follow the audio icons ◆ in the book to keep your spot on the CD. The track icons are placed after the figure numbers at the top of each figure. When more than one icon appears after a figure, the first track listed is a recording of the figure in full. All other track numbers listed are notable guitar parts played slower.

BAD LUCK SITUATION
(*Saints & Sinners*, 1974)
Written by Johnny Winter

Along with "Hurtin' So Bad," "Bad Luck Situation" was the only other original on Johnny Winter's follow up to *Still Alive and Well*. In addition, like his other albums from the early 1970s, it contained a fair portion of rock 'n' roll with the Stones' "Stray Cat Blues," Lieber and Stoller's "Riot in Cell Block #9," and Larry Williams' classic "Boney Moroney." Rick Derringer and the rest of the Johnny Winter And band of bassist Randy Jo Hobbs and drummer Richard Hughes, augmented by brother Edgar on keyboards and Dan Hartman on bass, among others, contributed mightily to the muscular release.

"Bad Luck Situation," performed as a trio with Hobbs and Hughes, is an infectious funk number that raises the question as to whether Winter had more in him like it, had he only been encouraged to write.

Figure 1—Intro

A prime slice of '70s funk gets "Bad Luck Situation" off to a booty-shaking start. Using the most minimal of melodic tools with the root, open position of the E minor pentatonic scale, and an E7 triple stop, Winter creates a cool head with bass lines, chords, and tightly syncopated rhythms in measures 1–4 before Hobbs and Hughes join in to help push the momentum forward to the verse.

Performance Tip: Use your index and middle fingers for the bass notes at frets 2 and 3, respectively. Play the E7 voicing with your middle, index, and ring fingers, low to high.

2 Full Band

3 Slow Demo
meas. 1-2, 8

Fig. 1

Intro 0:00

Funky blues-rock

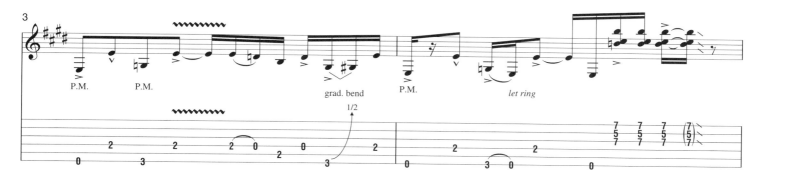

Published by WINTER BLUES MUSIC (BMI)

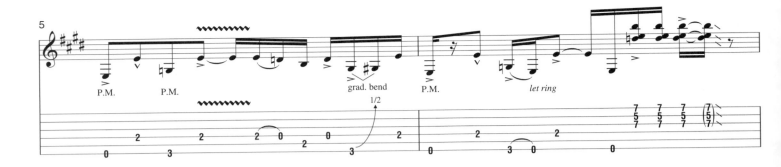

Figure 2—Verse

Winter combines the funk with the blues for a twelve-measure verse with the "slow IV chord change" (four measures of the I chord preceding the IV chord). Dig how he employs a modified version of the E minor pentatonic bass licks from the intro for measures 1–4 and 7–8, shifting to a modified boogie shuffle pattern for measures 5–6 over the A7 (IV) and then some rock-type power chords for measures 9 and 10 over the B (V) and A chord changes. These qualities sort of sum up of Winter's musical interests to date, which he follows with more of the funky stuff in measures 11–12 over the E7 change for a fine example of trio guitar playing. Observe how he inserts the G (♭7th) on fret 5 of string 4 on beat 4 of measures 5–6, without having it preceded by the F♯ (6th) note at fret 4, which would be the standard, blues-approved way to knock out a boogie pattern.

Performance Tip: Execute the double-string bend in measure 10 by pulling down with your index finger

4 **Full Band**

5 **Slow Demo** meas. 5-6, 9-10

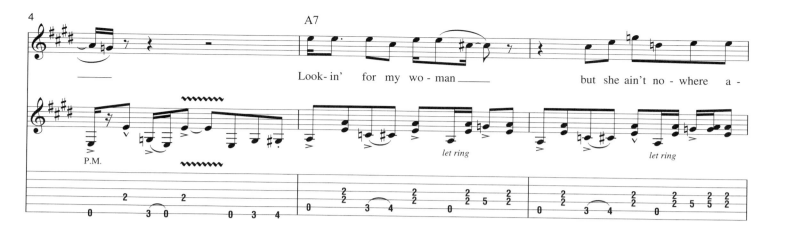

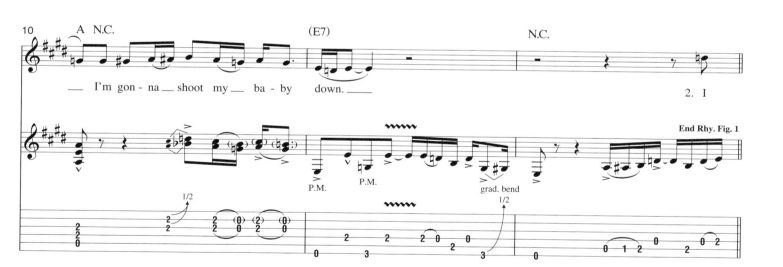

Figure 3—Guitar Solo

Two twelve-measure choruses similar to the verses provide the harmonic springboard for Winter to leap about in the root octave position of the E minor pentatonic scale. Running counter to the funky syncopation of the backing track, he cruises fluidly with high, arcing bends and greased-lightning triplets. The solo is a first-rate example of modal playing, with dynamic phrasing, contrasting textures, and careening momentum building musical tension combined with regular, though brief, resolution to the E (root) over the E (I) chord. Check out how he presents the modal concept immediately in measure 1 by beginning with a wicked, Albert King-type bend of two whole steps from G (♭3rd) to B (5th) followed by resolution to the E via a full-step bend from D (♭7th) to E on beat 4. In measure 2 he likewise creates tension with nasty bends to the B and D notes, while releasing it with repeated offerings of the E note in measure 3.

In measure 6 over the A (IV) chord, where resolution back to the E occurs naturally in measure 7, Winter ups the odds with unusual (for the blues) bends of the F♯ (6th) to G♯ (major 7th) and one last bend that goes all the way to A♯ (♭9th). Without skipping a beat (pun intended!) he continues with the over-extending bends in measure 7, whipping the F♯ (9th) up to B (5th). It is not until measure 11 that he nails the E (root) note with even a hint of resolution. And then, without pausing for so much as a breath, he is off and running in measure 12, carrying over his exuberance into measure 13 for the second blues chorus with similar bends.

In the second chorus Winter does lock deliberately into the harmony of the A (IV) change in measures 17–18 by riffing hard on D/B (4th/2nd) for tension with sixteenth-note triplets that evolve and resolve to C♯/A (3rd/root). Again, quick resolution to the E (root) over the E chord in measures 19–20 does occur, with the B (root) note being singled out for attention in measure 21 of the B (V) change. Tension is maintained in measure 22 over the A (IV) chord with the pot heated to a boil all the way through measures 23–24 over the E. Winter climaxes with that whopping two-step bend of G (♭3rd) to B on beat 4 of measure 24, as he did on beat 1 of measure 1 in the first chorus, bracketing his solo with a motif not often seen in the blues.

Performance Tip: Note Winter's use of a phase shifter, an effect he became enamored with around the release of *Saints & Sinners* that still catches his fancy to the present day. As perhaps the only major bluesman to incorporate the swirling sound into his music on a regular basis, it lends distinction to a style already predicated on uniqueness.

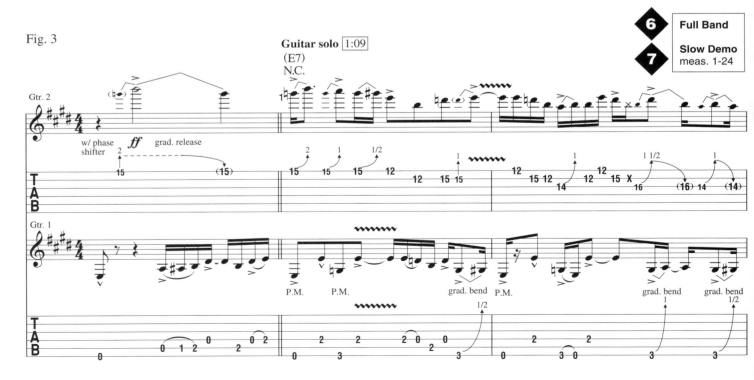

Fig. 3

Guitar solo 1:09

6 Full Band

7 Slow Demo meas. 1-24

12

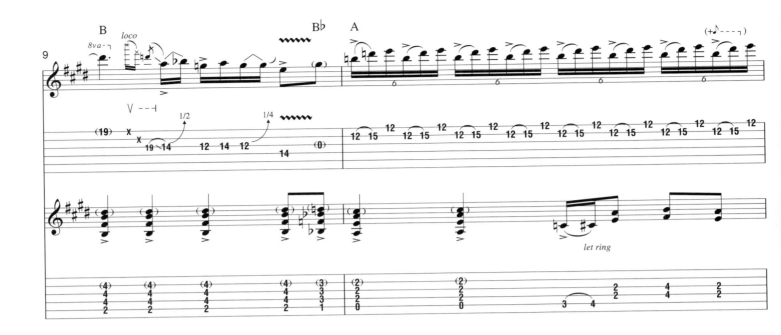

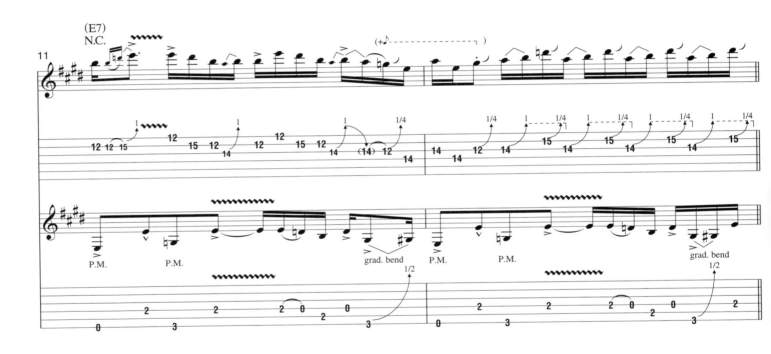

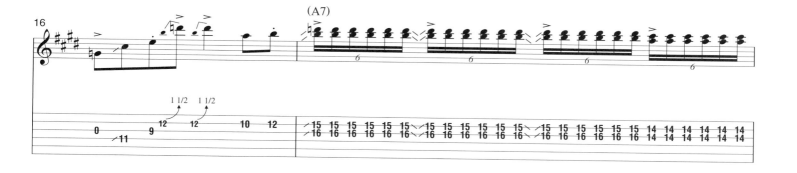

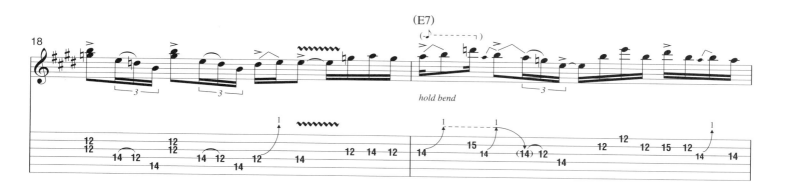

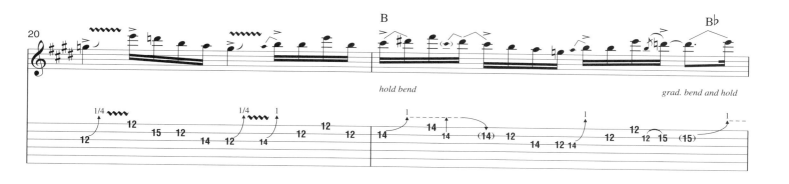

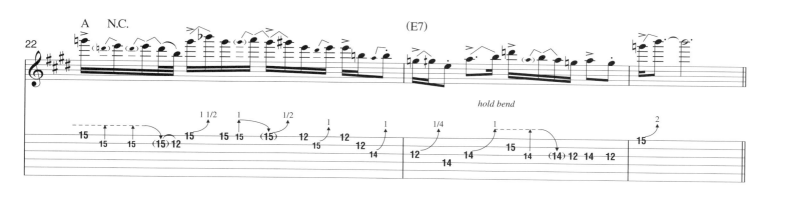

BE CAREFUL WITH A FOOL

(*Johnny Winter*, 1969)

Words and Music by B.B. King and Joe Bihari

The centerpiece of Johnny Winter's "official" debut album is a tour de force slow 12-bar blues. With the exuberance of youth and chops that can only be called superhuman, he tears through the B.B. King classic on a weird Fender XII twelve-string solid body axe converted to six strings.

Figure 4—Verse 2

Winter fills like a "fool" throughout, but in verse 2 with the "fast IV change" (one measure of the I chord preceding the IV chord) he kicks it off with a classic triple-stop pattern likely learned from his idol Muddy Waters, who in turn probably gleaned it from Robert Johnson. Be aware that E/Bb/G (3rd/b7th/5th) in measure 1 on the C7 (I) chord indicates the dominant tonality, while the same voicing one fret lower in measure 2 over the F7 (IV) change implies a dominant b9 tonality with Eb/A/F# (b7th/3rd/b9th). After employing the open-position C minor pentatonic scale in measures 3–4, with emphasis on the C (root) note, he follows in measure 5 over the F7 chord with a usual triple stop of C/Eb/F (5th/b7th/root) to reinforce the tonality. From there on, however, Winter is more judicious with his note selection as regards "target notes," dyads, or triple stops to help define the chord changes. For instance, in measure 10 over the F change he lays on the Eb (b7th), in measure 7 over C7 chord he executes a unison bend on the Bb (b7th) notes, while on beats 3–4 in measure 12 he outlines the G7#9 chord with the G (root), F (b7th), and Bb (#9th) notes.

Performance Tip: To efficiently access the triple stop in measure 4, slide up to fret 8 on string 5 with your index finger and then place your middle and ring fingers on strings 3 and 1, respectively.

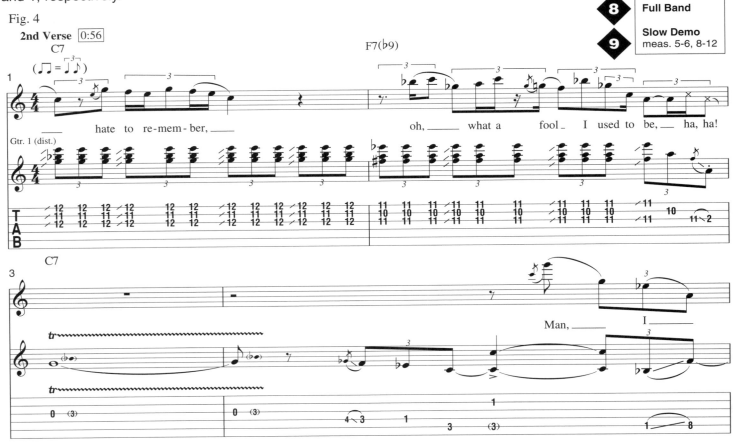

Figure 5—Guitar Solo

What is most amazing about Winter's three-chorus solo masterpiece is not the jaw-dropping technique, but the way he is able to maintain and build interest while playing modally as if his life depended on it. Though there are dynamic rests along the way scattered like so many drops of rain in the desert, for the most part it is a torrential downpour of eighth, sixteenth, and thirty-second notes that fall from his fingers.

Not surprisingly, the first chorus finds Winter laying it down almost exclusively in the root position of the C minor pentatonic scale at fret 8. Virtually every measure sounds as though he has taken a deep breath and then lets the notes fly out in a rush that slows perceptively to beat 4 in what is accepted as authentic electric blues phrasing from the style of B.B. King on. The exceptions occur in measures 3, 11, and 12 where he presents a classic blues dyad of Bb/G (b7th/5th) to either complement the dominant tonality (measures 3 and 11 over the C7 chord) or create tension (beats 3–4 of measure 12 over the G7 chord). Measure 9 contains both concepts as Winter hammers from the F (b7th) to the G (root) bass notes over the G7 (V) chord. Be sure to pay attention to the way Winter connects the dyads at the end of the first chorus to the unison bend in measure 13 (also found in measure 7 of verse 2) in order to advance the tune and up the energy ante.

In chorus 2 Winter begins his ascent to the realm of the blues gods above the clouds. After maintaining momentum with the Bb (b7th of C, 4th of F) unison bend in measures 13–14 over the I–IV change, he works in the Bb/G (b7th/5th) dyad that implies a C7 tonality to go with the C7 chord in measure 15. In measure 16, however, he leaps to the fifteenth position for a startling and dynamic shift in register and begins adding in scalding bursts of notes through to the end of the chorus in several positions of the C minor pentatonic scale. Observe how he strikes the C (5th) and Eb (b7th) notes over the F7 (IV) chord in measure 17 to emphasize the dominant tonality while prominently nicking the G (root) note in measure 21 over the G7 (V) chord. Though fairly rare occurrences, these "target notes" contribute to the logic of his note choice among the blizzard of other less specific scale tones. Then, as he did between measure 12 and 13, Winter connects the second and third choruses with a repeating lick. In this case, it is a slippery gliss on string 2 to fret 20 that combines with fret 18 on string 1 to produce Bb/G, which functions as b3rd/root over the G7 and b7th/5th over the C7.

Where a lesser blues guitar hero (they know who they are!) would have gone flat out during their climactic chorus with high-register, high-speed riffing, Winter takes a different, more authentic-to-the-genre approach. Between measures 28–32, he actually finds his way back down the fingerboard, ending up in the open position of the C minor pentatonic scale in measures 31–32 for a breath-taking, dynamic drop in register. Of course, he still continues to twist the neck of his axe into a pretzel with rocketing bends and serpentine hammers and pulls combining the open G (5th) string and the Bb (b7th) note on fret 3 in measures 31–32.

In measure 33 over the G7 chord he pulls a real surprise by literally moving to the root position of the G minor pentatonic scale at fret 3 as he "plays the change" instead of proceeding modally in the C minor pentatonic scale as he has done throughout. The move lends distinction as well as concrete structure to the progression, as does the G (root), F (b7th), and Bb(#9) notes over beats 3–4 of the G7#9 chord in measure 36 for closure.

Performance Tip: Play the repeating triplets in measure 24 in chorus 2 and measure 25 in chorus 3 by sliding on string 2 from fret 18 (F) to 20 (G) with your ring finger. Access the Bb note at fret 18 on string 1 with your index finger.

Fig. 5

* Played behind the beat.

hold bend

19

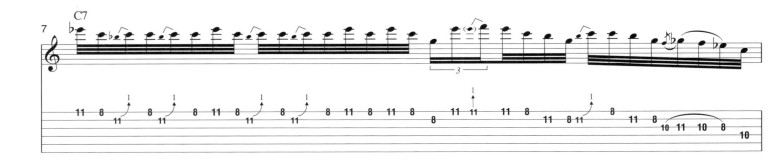

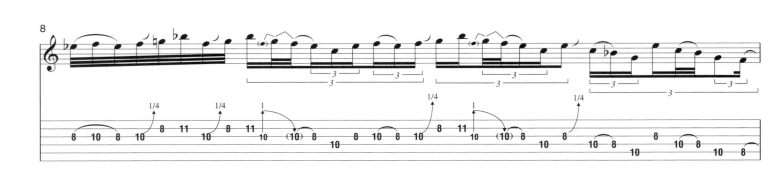

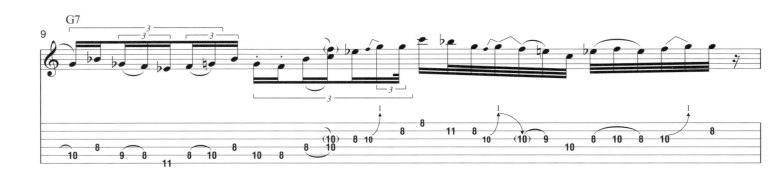

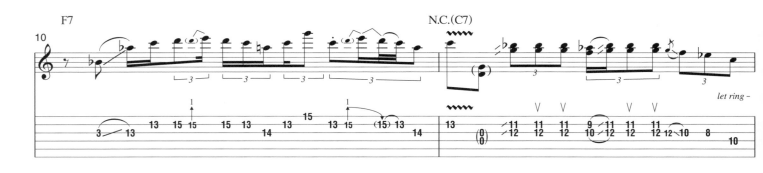

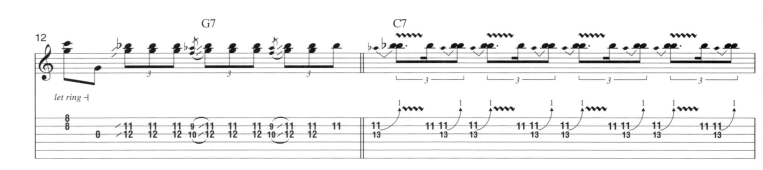

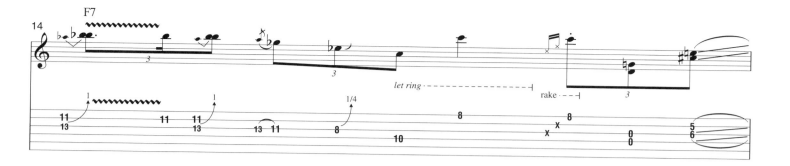

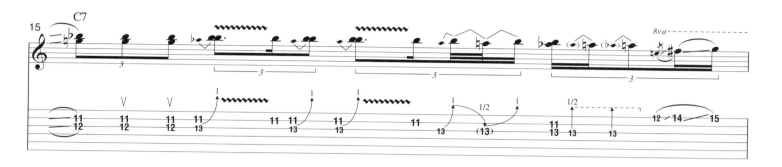

* Played behind the beat.

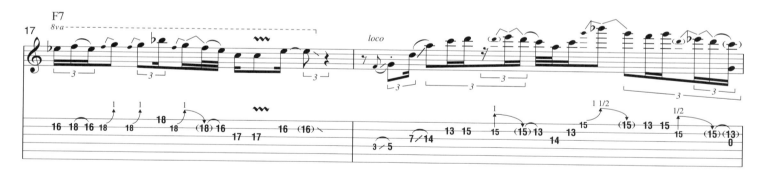

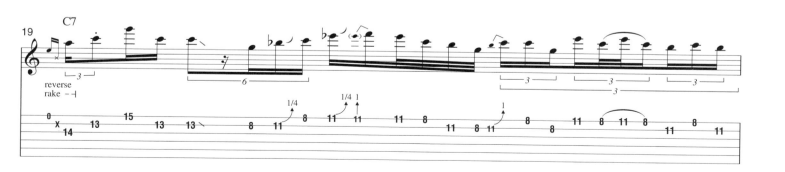

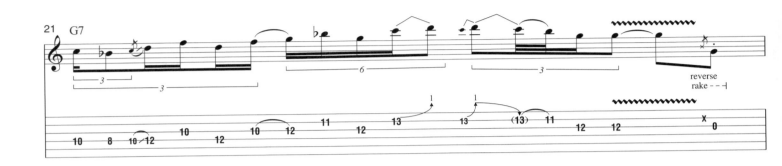

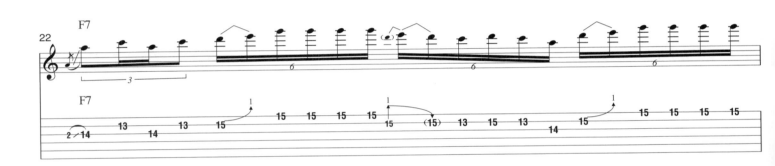

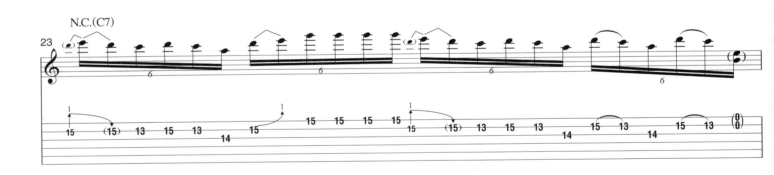

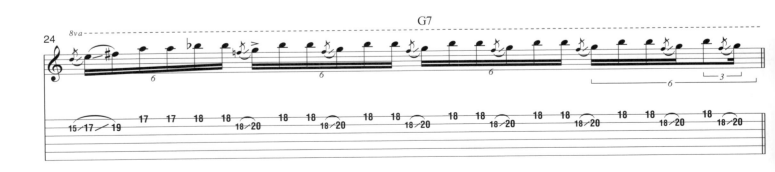

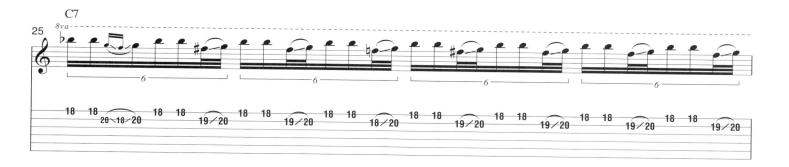

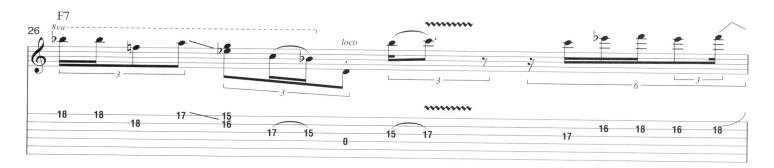

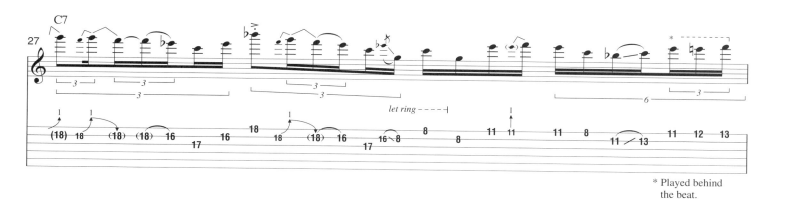

* Played behind
  the beat.

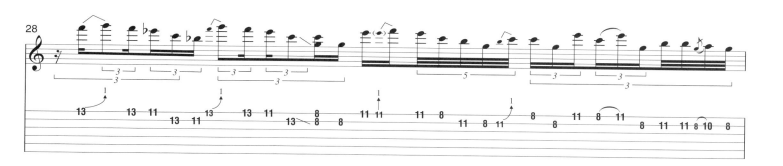

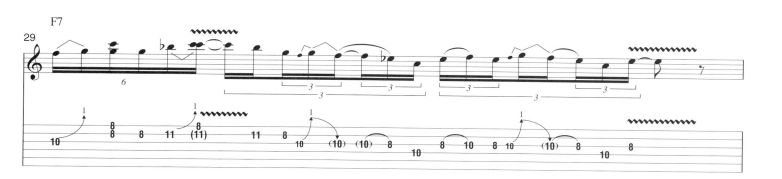

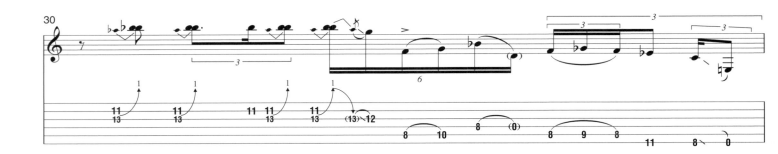

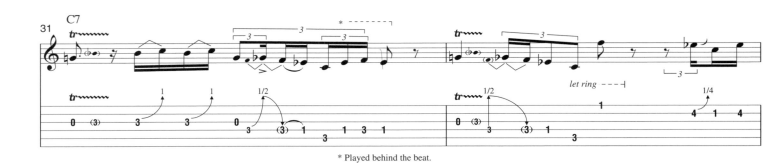

*Played behind the beat.

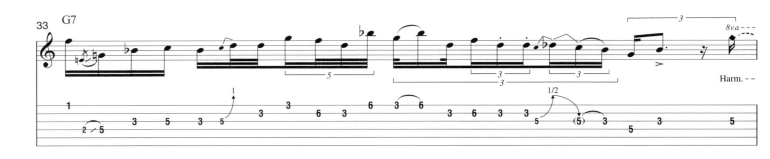

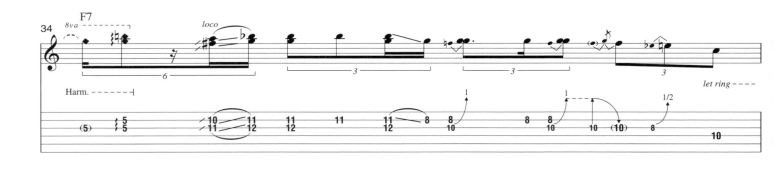

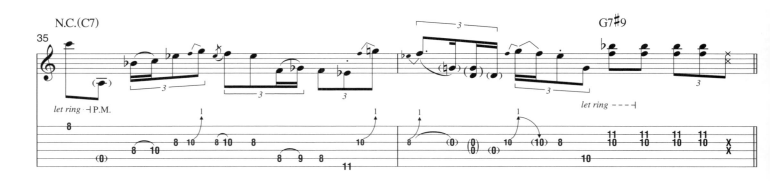

BLADIE MAE
(*Nothin' But the Blues*, 1977)
Written by Johnny Winter

Johnny Winter's "all blues, all the time" release must have come as somewhat of a shock to his younger fans that were digging on the rock he had been playing with gusto since the early 1970s. However, it was a watershed event in his career followed by a second blues album and his justly lauded collaboration with Muddy at the end of the decade. "Bladie Mae" takes it all the way back home with Winter's golden slide touch on the National Steel.

Figure 6—Verse 1

Winter (Gtr. 1) tunes his acoustic metal axe to open G and places a capo on fret 3 while second guitarist Bob Margolin (Gtr. 2) places a capo on fret 1 for the twelve-measure slow blues with the "slow IV change." For the most part, Gtr. 2 plays boogie patterns and bass lines with subtle embellishments.

Gtr. 1, as is the custom when playing slide, particularly in open tuning, follows the I–IV–V chord changes with the appropriate notes and chord positions. Observe how he frets 5th/♭7th at fret 3 (measures 1–2), ♭3rd/♭7th at fret 3 (measure 7), uses the slide at fret 12 (measure 3) along with the open strings for the I chord, and moves the slide to fret 5 (measure 6) for the IV chord. A cool fingered root/♭7th/5th implies V in measure 9. Adding appropriate blues spice is the ♭7th note played over the IV chord in measure 5.

Performance Tip: Real blues cats wear the slider on their pinky so they can fret with the other three fingers. Hence, the V7 voicing in measure 9 should be played with your middle and first fingers, low to high.

Fig. 6

Gtr. 1: Open G tuning, capo III:
(low to high) D–G–D–G–B–D

Gtr. 2: Capo I

12 Full Band

13 Slow Demo
Gtr. 1 meas. 3-4, 7-8, 10-12

1st Verse [0:14]

Moderately slow Blues ♩ = 73

Y'-know I got a brand new friend, an' I calls her Blad-ie

*Symbols in parentheses represent chord names respective to capoed Gtr. 1. Symbols in double parentheses represent chord names respective to capoed Gtr. 2. Symbols above reflect actual sounding chords. Capoed frets are "0" in tab.

Published by WINTER BLUES MUSIC (BMI)
All Rights Reserved   Used by Permission

Figure 7—Guitar Solo

Two twelve-measure choruses provide Winter with a fine opportunity to show how he absorbed the tradition of acoustic country blues emanating from Charlie Patton through Son House to Robert Johnson and Muddy Waters. He eases into the first chorus by incorporating several musical ideas from verse 1, but starts to open it up in measure 4 when he dynamically leaps to the root octave position at fret 12 with the F (5th), D (3rd), and B♭ (root) notes outlining the B♭ major triad. Continuing with the concept of following the harmonic changes, Winter nails the tonality with B♭/G (5th/3rd) over the E♭ (IV) on beat 1 of measure 5. On beat 7, however, he emphasizes D♭/B♭ (♭7th/5th) at fret 8 to create musical tension and is off and running, producing more tension and resolution, mostly with single notes. Observe the hot slide lick of D (3rd) to B♭ (root as string 3 open) in measures 7–8 over the B♭ (I) change.

The second chorus has Winter playing more energetically, especially in the lower positions where he incorporates open strings into his licks for a bracing shot of dynamics. Notice how this approach is exceptionally effective in measure 14 over the B♭ (I) chord as he inserts the open B♭ (string 3) following the fretted B♭ on beat 1, the open B♭ (string 3) following the fretted D (3rd) on beat 5, the open F (string 4 functioning as the 5th) following the A♭ (♭7th) on beat 8, and the open B♭ (string 5) following D on beat 12. The way he bangs out sixteenth notes on the open third string in measure 15 makes for a powerful buildup to the A♭/F (♭7th/5th) dyad in measure 16 that supports the B♭ tonality.

Warming to the task, Winter builds a head of steam with ringing dyads in measures 17–19. The octave of A♭/F (♭7th/5th) clangs as the climax of the solo on beat 6 of measure 19, resolving to the B♭ triad at the twelfth fret of F/D/B♭ (5th/3rd/root), and then to strings 2 (D), 3 (B♭), and 4 (F) open on beat 12. In measure 20 he drops precipitously to the lower register and womps on A/D (major 7th/3rd) and B♭/E♭ (root/4th) to expand the B♭ tonality in a manner similar to House and Waters. Winding down to a satisfying conclusion, he slithers around on the bass strings confirming tonality with A♭ (♭3rd), A (3rd), and F (root) over F (V) in measure 21, the E♭ (root) and B♭ (5th) over E♭ (IV) in measure 22, and the B♭ (root), E♭ (4th), D (3rd), and A♭ (♭7th) over B♭ (I) in measure 23. Heavy emphasis on B♭ (string 5 open) and F (string 6 open) wraps up the I and V changes in measure 24.

Performance Tip: Quarter-step notes indicated in measures 2 and 9 in the first chorus and measures 13, 17, 19, 21 and 23 in the second chorus should be accessed by sliding slightly past the targeted fret position for the real deal funk!

Fig. 7

Guitar Solo 1:33

14 Full Band

15 Slow Demo
Gtr. 1   meas. 2,4
7-12, 14-15, 20-22

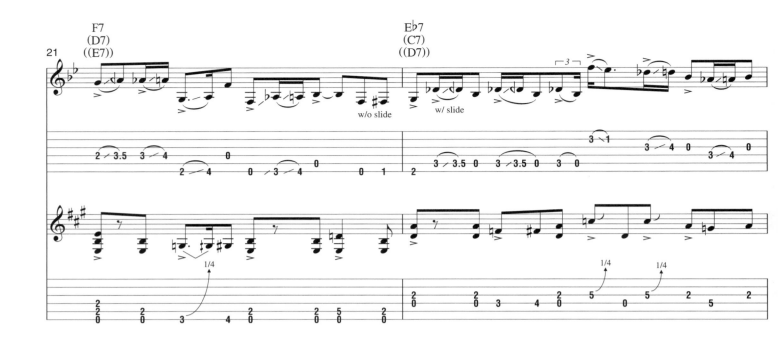

HIGHWAY 61 REVISITED
(*Second Winter*,1969)
Words and Music by Bob Dylan

The highlight of Johnny Winter's official sophomore effort, Dylan's classic from his self-titled 1965 album, is turned into a slide guitar tour-de-force. *Second Winter* is not generally regarded as essential listening, despite Edgar's sympathetic backing and the novelty that it was originally a three-sided vinyl release. Nonetheless, "Highway 61 Revisited" remains a cornerstone of Winter's live performances and a fan favorite. It also makes a connection back to one of Winter's early supporters, Mike Bloomfield, who played guitar on the Dylan original.

Figure 8—Intro

Four measures of D7 (I) are all Winter needs to set the "tone" (literally and figuratively) of his open D tuning romp. Naturally, D/A (root/5th) at fret 12 in measures 1–2 establish the D major tonality while C (♭7th) and A (5th) at fret 15 in measure 3 imply the dominant tonality of the blues. Measure 4 contains a tart run down the D blues scale that begins on D/B (root/6th) for an implied D6 tonality, and ends on A for consonance as a lead in to D/A in verse 1 (not shown).

Performance Tip: Winter wears a thumbpick that helps give him exceptional down and up picking technique that is required, for example, to play the licks in measure 3. Nonetheless, a flatpick will do just as well, as will bare fingers like the thumb and index.

Figure 9—Verse 5

Like many of Dylan's tunes from the mid to late 1960s, "Highway 61 Revisited" is a lengthy composition. Based on standard blues changes, if not the standard 12-bar form, it moves from D7 (I) for eight measures to G7 (IV) for two measures, through four measures of D7, two measures of A7 (V), and finishes with two measures of D7 (a total of eighteen measures). Be aware that additional instrumental measures from eight to fifteen are tacked on at the end of each verse. Verse 5, the last verse, actually segues seamlessly into an extra thirty-four measures to the fade that function as a coda and de facto guitar solo.

During his vocal, Winter mainly follows the changes by relocating to the fret position that coincides with the chords. As is the procedure for not only open D, but open G tuning as well, this involves employing the open strings or the octave at fret 12 for the I chord, fret 5 for the IV chord, and fret 7 for the V chord. For the most part, Winter follows this program with few exceptions, such as in measures 7 and 17–18 over the D7 (I) chord, where he whips up to C/A (♭7th/5th) at fret 15 to imply the dominant tonality, not present with the open strings or at fret 12. Not coincidentally, measure 18 transitions to the solo where Winter gives a master class in modal improvisation with the type of skill that only comes through the experience of extended listening and playing. Be aware that it is "art," not "science," and that there is no way to accomplish the desired effect by counting the measures of musical tension and release to find a system that does not exist.

Winter creates tension in a variety of dynamic ways. In measures 19–20 he slashes through with a triplet containing the notes A/F/C (5th/♭3rd/♭7th), with the ♭3rd adding some "blues grit," and then begins a concentrated run of resolution starting in measure 21 with the D (root) note. Continuing through to measure 28, he regularly inserts the open first and second strings (A and D) for release, sliding into assorted D minor pentatonic notes for contrast and brief tension. Measures 29–32 find Winter zooming up the neck in a breathtaking show of musical muscle to produce a climax of startling tension starting with the dominant tonality of C/A (♭7th/5th) and moving to D/B (root/6th), F/D (♭3rd/root), and finally G/E (4th/9th) at fret 24.

Quite logically, Winter returns to resolution leavened with D minor pentatonic notes and dyads beginning in measure 33 with a dramatic and dynamic drop in register going all the way through to the fade in measure 52. Be sure to see the raspy "blues note" of the F (♭3rd) on string 1 at fret 3 in measure 33 that Winter vibratos with gusto. As he takes his solo out, Winter engages heavily in a technique hinted at earlier in the song: He plays open strings in virtually every measure, often placing them dynamically along side upper register notes and licks for maximum effect. No where is this more apparent than in measures 37–39 where he jumps between fret positions on string 1 while pulling off to the open (D) string with a series of roiling triplets. A similar concept leads to the fade in measures 51–52 where Winter again employs triplets as he alternates between string 1 open (D) and the fretted D at fret 5 for conclusive resolution on the root.

Performance Tip: The biggest challenge in playing slide is in executing clean, fast runs down the scale (or fret position) as in measure 40. Right and left hand muting in between each note is crucial. Work slowly and methodically at acquiring this skill, making sure to quickly and adroitly drop the heel of your right hand down on the bridge of your guitar as you lift the slide to go to the next note, particularly when shifting from one string to another.

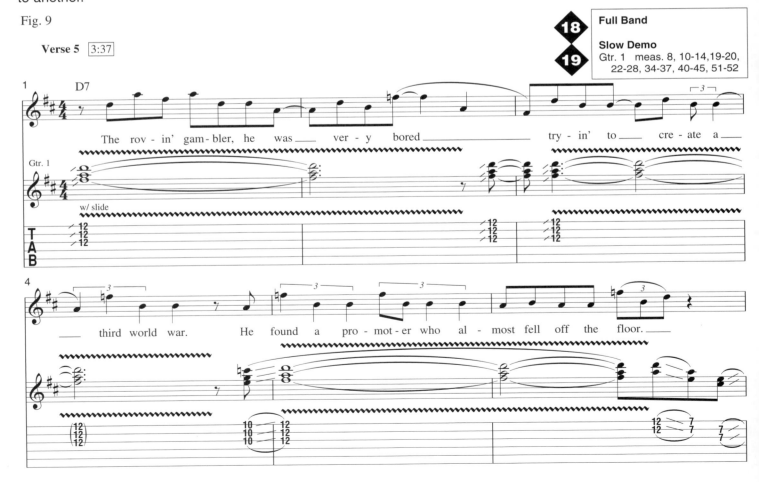

Fig. 9

Verse 5 3:37

18 / 19 Full Band

Slow Demo
Gtr. 1 meas. 8, 10-14,19-20, 22-28, 34-37, 40-45, 51-52

D7

The rov - in' gam - bler, he was ___ ver - y bored _____ try - in' to ___ cre - ate a ___

Gtr. 1

w/ slide

___ third world war. He found a pro - mot - er who al - most fell off the floor. ____

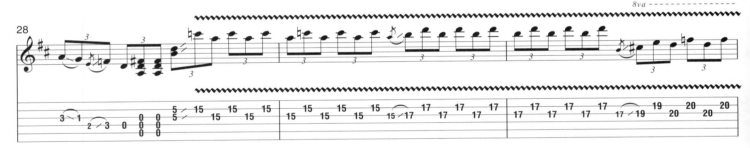

IT WAS RAINING
(*Nothin' But the Blues*, 1977)
Written by Johnny Winter

It was a short step from Johnny Winter being backed by the Muddy Waters band in 1977 to Johnny Winter producing and playing on Muddy Waters's *Hard Again* with the same personnel the same year. In fact, "It Was Raining" bears a passing resemblance to Waters's "Deep Down in Florida" on *Hard Again* and is one of the most authentic down home blues Winter has ever recorded.

Figure 10—Intro

This slow twelve-bar blues is constructed upon a lazy, altered boogie bass line played by Winter as first shown in the intro. The A (I), D (IV), and E (V) chord changes are relatively identical, with a classic two-note pick up of the ♭3rd to major 3rd (C–C♯, F–F♯, and G–G♯ for the A, D, and E chord changes, respectively) leading into the down beat of each change. See how the riff incorporates the root, ♭7th (bent a quarter step to the "true blue note" between the ♭7th and major 7th) and 5th notes of each chord change for the appropriate dominant tonality. Note also that the intro contains the "slow IV change," while the verses (not shown) contain the "fast IV change."

Performance Tip: Play the bend in each measure with your ring finger backed up by the middle and index fingers

Fig. 10

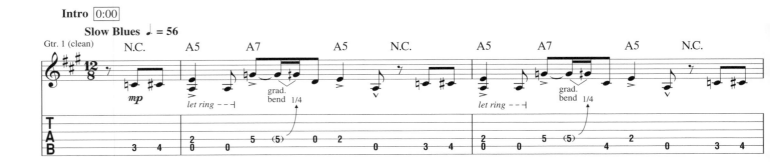

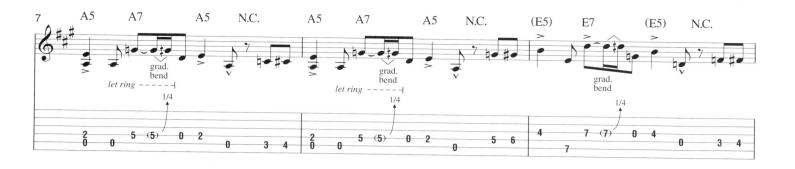

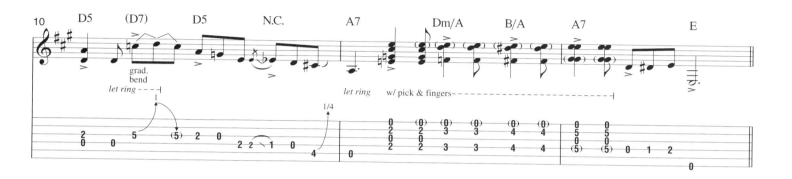

Figure 11–Guitar Solo

Deviating substantially from the "down home blues tradition" of the accompaniment, but playing firmly in the "Johnny Winter soloing tradition," the artist rips through two twelve-measure choruses like a coyote through a flock of sheep. As is usually his wont, he basically winds his way through the A minor pentatonic scale at all fret positions, with the occasional ♭5th (E♭) "blues note" inserted to turn the minor pentatonic into the blues scale. As is also his modus operandi, he takes a strictly modal approach, building tension through a variety of guitaristic means and releasing it to the A note that functions as the root of A (I) and the 5th of D (IV). When he plays the A note over the E (V) chord, however, it creates musical tension as the suspended 4th that needs to be released in the succeeding measure, be it the D in measure 10 or the A in the next 12-bar chorus.

Winter produces most of his musical tension through any number of bends that appear in virtually every measure. Measure 1 in the first blues chorus is a perfect example, where he bends the G (♭7th) on string 2 up a half-step to the G♯ (major 7th) on the way to the A (root). In addition, he also bends the D (4th) on string 3 one step to the E (5th), along with the C (♭3rd) a quarter step to the "blue note" in between the ♭3rd and major 3rd (C♯). In measure 2 he "finds a home" with the D note on string 3 and executes a series of quarter-step and whole-step bends for a vocal-like effect. With a dynamic leap in register in measure 4 Winter presents a similar concept at fret 15 on string 1 where he bends and releases the G (♭7th) repeatedly in a soaring display of articulation. He closes out the first chorus in measure 12 over the A (I) and E (V) changes with a classic double-string bend of C/F♯ (♭3rd/6th over A, ♭6th/9th over E) up a quarter step in a move that T-Bone Walker passed down to Chuck Berry, among others. Observe how the D (4th of A, ♭7th of E) is included in the equation starting on beat 2 and that it is bent a half step along with the F♯ to form a triple-stop of C/G/E♭ (E♭ functioning as the bluesy ♭5th of A and the major 7th of E). The tension created by this move is almost physically palpable and creates terrific momentum going into the next chorus.

The second chorus kicks off in measure 13 with another classic riff via the A dominant triple-stop of C♯/G/E (3rd/♭7th/5th) that Lonnie Johnson, Robert Johnson, and Muddy Waters popularized. Do not miss how Winter, in measure 14, moves it down the neck to imply A°7 and A♭°7, and then back up to A°7 and A7 in measure 15. He then creates anticipation by moving 6ths up the neck, implying A♯7 and B7 before resolving in measure 16 to an implied A13 and an A9 triple stop, and then runs in the A Mixolydian mode with emphasis on the A (root) notes. Be aware that including these forms contributes structure and logic to Winter's solo, adds dynamic contrast to his fast, improvised scale work, and makes a connection back to the pre-war roots of modern blues.

Winter completes his power-packed, headlong rush to the finish line of the second chorus in similar fashion to the first with speedy licks and punchy bends in the A minor pentatonic scale. However, in measure 22 over the D7 (IV) chord, he dips into the D Mixolydian mode for beats 1–6 for a surprising moment of "playing the changes" rather than modal improvisation. Dig how he resolves with great finality in measure 24 with fretted A (root) notes, the G (♭7th) bent one step up to A, and the fretted A on string 4 closing the show.

Performance Tip: Use your ring and pinky fingers, low to high, for the double- and triple-string bends in measure 12. Check out that you have to catch string 3 under your ring finger along with string 2, a sometimes tricky proposition at best. Try it with your thumb hooked over the top edge of the fingerboard so that your ring finger approaches strings 2 and 3 at a very flat angle, making it easier for string 3 to slide underneath while you apply considerable pressure.

Fig. 11

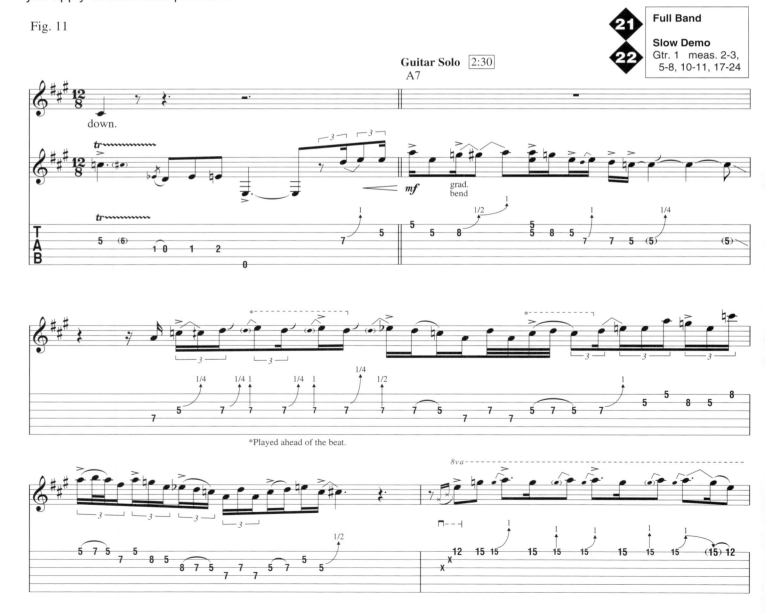

Guitar Solo 2:30
A7

*Played ahead of the beat.

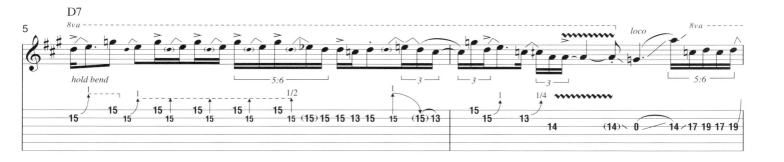

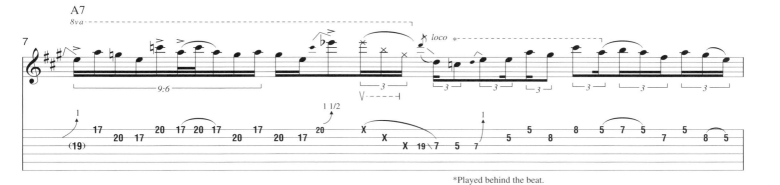

*Played behind the beat.

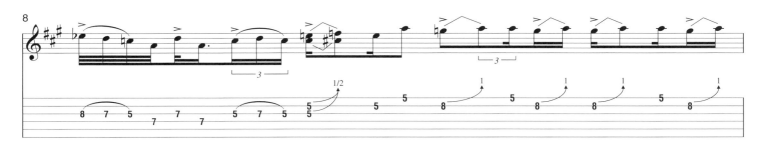

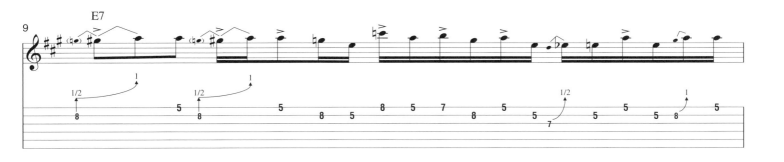

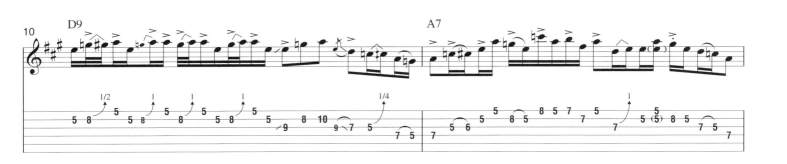

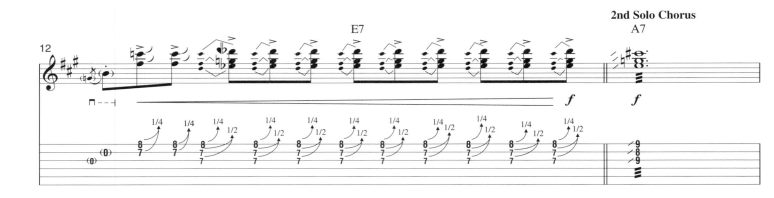

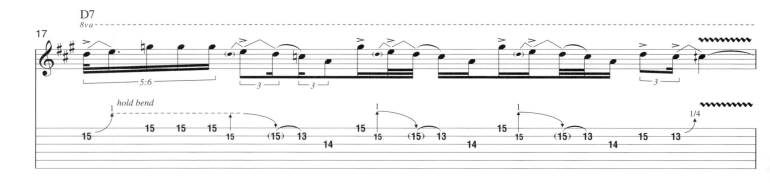

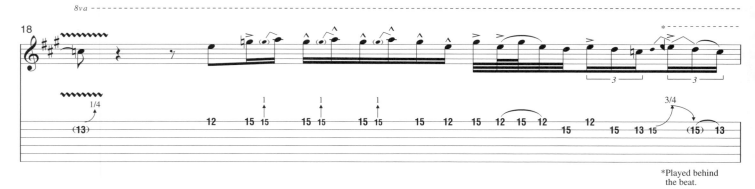

*Played behind
the beat.

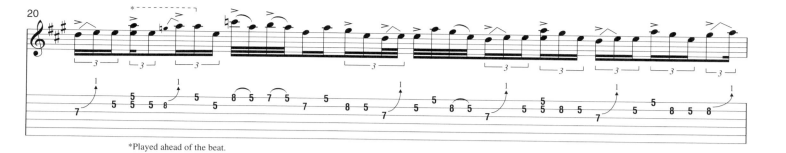

*Played ahead of the beat.

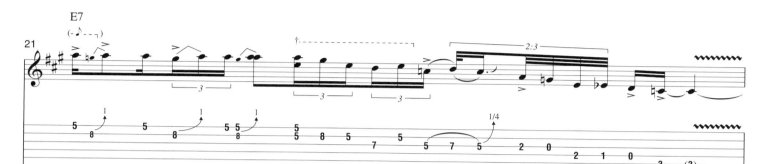

†Played behind the beat.

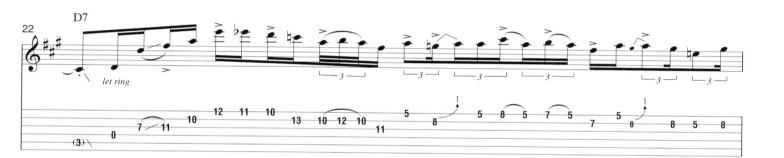

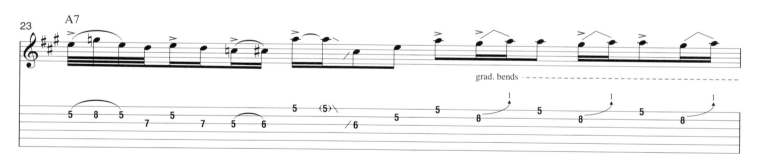

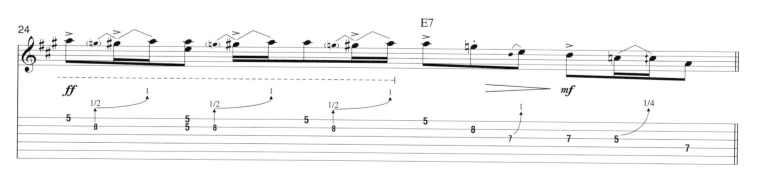

LELAND MISSISSIPPI
(*Johnny Winter*, 1969)
Written by Johnny Winter

The chord progression and feel of "Leland Mississippi" is reminiscent of B.B. King's "Rock Me Baby" as well as, surprisingly, the Rolling Stones' "Parachute Woman" from *Beggar's Banquet* (1968). It is a groove Johnny Winter has favored during his long career, providing ample opportunity for his dead-on "call and response" fills. In addition, it also allows this true "son of the Delta" to pay homage to his birthplace.

Figure 12—Intro

Lifting a page from the Muddy Waters songbook with a riff similar to "Rolling Stone" and "Still a Fool," Winter conjures a dramatic and classic-sounding country blues intro in measures 3–6. Observe that it is the only section of the tune that starts on the E7 (I) chord.

Fig. 12

Intro

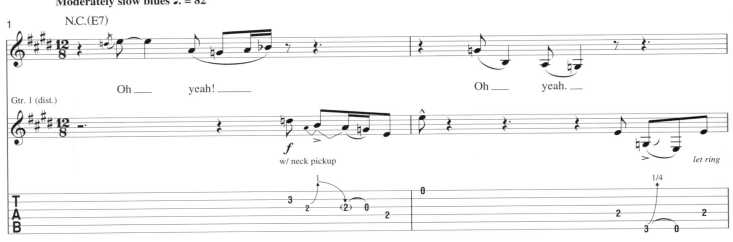

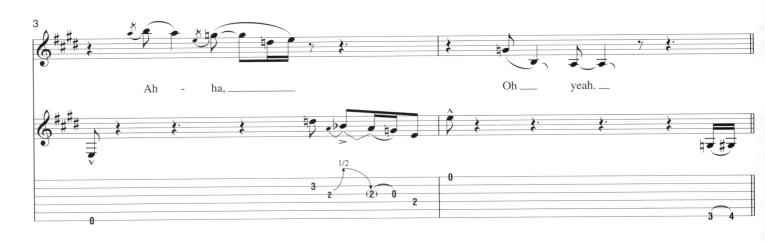

Published by WINTER BLUES MUSIC (BMI)

Figure 13—Verse 2

Each verse is fourteen measures long with A7 (IV), A7, E7 (I), E7, E7, A7, A7, E7, E7, E7, B7 (V), A7, E7, and E7 changes. Beginning on the IV chord is unusual enough in the blues, but having three measures of the I chord in a row makes the progression rather unique and gives it kinship with prewar country blues that often had odd numbers of measures or even beats. Somehow, Winter makes his composition sound completely natural, however, which is a testament to his command of the blues form.

Measures 1–2, 6–7, and 11–12 of the A (IV) chord are the "call" with Winter singing in unison with his guitar licks. Measures 3–5, 8–10, and 13–14 contain the "response" with improvised licks. The combination makes for an exciting dynamic that creates an endless cycle of chords with continuous momentum. Check out how Winter switches from the E minor pentatonic scale to the A Mixolydian mode in measures 1, 6, and 7 of the A7 (IV) chord, with the C♯ (major 3rd) defining the major tonality of the changes. Understand that the Mixolydian mode is the "dominant" mode, or scale, and therefore the right choice for the blues. In addition, be sure to see how Winter uses the A (♭7th), F♯ (5th, bent from the E, or 4th), and B (root) notes from the E minor pentatonic scale in measure 11 of the B7 (V) chord to nail the tonality.

Performance Tip: The classic blues lick on beat 10 of measure 4 of the E7 (I) change should be played by barring at fret 14 with your ring finger, then quickly barring at fret 12 with your index finger and hammering to fret 13 on string 3 with your middle finger. The similar lick an octave lower in measure 9 should be trilled with the middle finger.

Fig. 13

Figure 14—Guitar Solo

Winter keeps the ball rolling by charging headlong into the solo with the same chord progression as the verses. Dig how he "plays the changes" with more frequency, however, than in the verses where his approach is mostly modal with various forms of tension and release. In measures 1 and 6 over the A7 (IV) chord, he employs G/E (♭7th/5th) to imply the A7 tonality. For most of the E (I) changes, he mainly wends his way through the root position of the E minor pentatonic scale save for measure 8, where he relocates to the twelfth position and the root octave box of the scale for dynamic contrast to the low, growly bass licks and runs. Over the B7 (V) change in measure 11, he uses the dyad form from measures 1 and 6, but moves them up the fingerboard two frets to become A/F♯ (♭7th/5th) before clearly defining the B tonality with the classic blues lick from measure 4 of verse 2 moved appropriately to fret 7 and the root position box of the B pentatonic scale. On beats 1–4 in measure 12, Winter makes a surprise move with a unison bend at fret 3 of the G (♭7th) notes over A7 (IV). He then smoothly transitions to the root open position of the E minor pentatonic scale on beats 5–12 of the measure in anticipation of the E7 (I) change in measure 13.

Performance Tip: Execute the double-string bend in measure 8 by pulling down with your ring finger. Likewise, pull down on the following G (♭7th) note at fret 12 on string 3 with your index finger.

Fig. 14

26 Full Band

27 Slow Demo
meas. 6-8, 10-12

Guitar Solo `1:32`

MEAN TOWN BLUES
(*The Progressive Blues Experiment*, 1969)
Words and Music by Johnny Winter

The "black sheep" of Johnny Winter's early releases that he has described as "live without an audience," *The Progressive Blues Experiment* includes classics like "Rollin' And Tumblin'," "Help Me," "It's My Own Fault," "Forty-Four" and a future classic from his own hand. "Mean Town Blues" is a down and dirty tour de force boogie number in open A tuning that was one of the first of his tracks to reveal his monster slide chops. It is also worth noting that open A was a favorite of Robert Johnson, one of Winter's main slide influences.

Figure 15—Intro

Though Winter is tuned to open A in the manner of the original Boogie Man, John Lee Hooker, "Mean Town Blues" actually shows a closer affinity to Magic Sam's "I Feel So Good (I Wanna Boogie)" in standard tuning from 1967. The similarity only goes so far, however, as Winter puts his own personal stamp on the style with "Texas twang" in the four measures of Rhy. Fig. 1 that drive the song.

Performance Tip: It is highly recommended to play "Mean Town Blues" fingerstyle throughout. Try plucking with your thumb (Winter uses a plastic thumbpick) for the bass licks on strings 6 and 5 and string 5 open (A). Use your index finger for string 3 (A) open and for the double-stop of strings 4 (E) and 3 open.

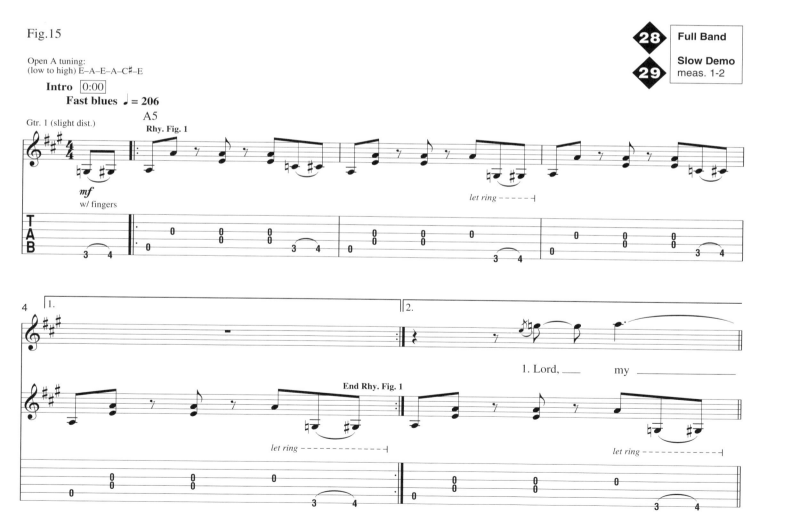

Figure 16—Verse

The thirty-measure verse is composed of several riffs strung together, and those in measures 7–12 and 21–26 that add welcome dynamic contrast to the relentlessly churning boogie patterns throughout the song. Notice how the unison vocal/guitar line in measures 27–28 gives the impression that "time" is slowing down.

"Mean Town Blues" is a totally modal I-chord boogie in A major with the G (♭7th) and C (♭3rd) notes added from the A minor pentatonic scale for the "blues" vibe. They are most prominent in the instrumental "interlude" of measures 7–12 and 21–26.

Performance Tip: Dig that the guitar melody line in measures 27–28 is played with the slide. "Real bluesmen" (or blueswomen) always wear their slides on the pinky so that the other three fingers are free for conventional fretting.

mother,_____ she done told me and_____ my   fa - ther done

told   me,_____   my_____ fa - ther told_____ me,   too._____

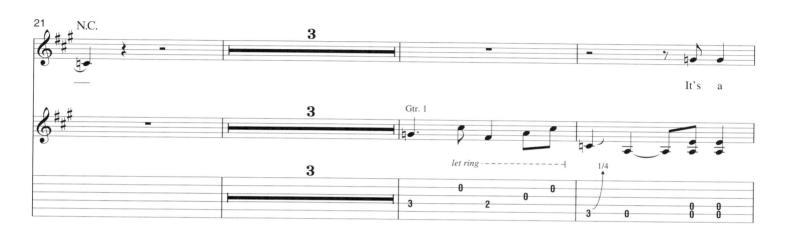

It's a

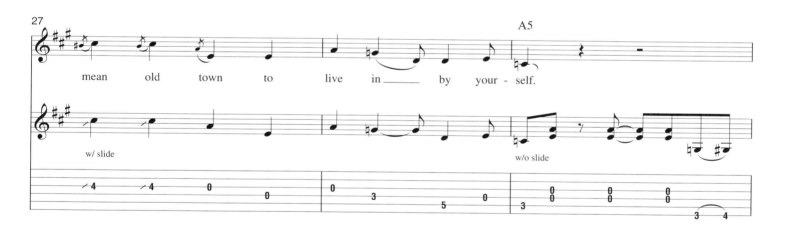

mean   old   town   to   live   in _____ by   your - self.

2. Yeah, I_____

Figure 17—Guitar Solo

Though not of the epic proportions it would take on in live performances and recordings in the 1970s, the solo for "Mean Town Blues" is still a lengthy excursion where few had gone before. Winter is a master of modal playing over I, IV, and V changes, but here he also proves his worth over a static I (A) chord change. Making it even more of a challenge to hold the listener's interest for eighty-seven measures of improvisation is the fact that Winter only has Uncle John Turner's kick drum for accompaniment through the solo as Tommy Shannon "strolls" with the bass. To say that he succeeds admirably is an understatement.

He starts off without the slide in root position, and spends most of his time mining the first five frets for gems of the genre. However, he also spans a full octave to fret 12 and beyond in a virtuosic display incapable of being duplicated by most other guitarists "back in the day," save for Duane Allman. Perhaps because he is providing all the harmony and melody, he never strays far from the open strings, using string 3 (A, the root) literally as a pedal point in measures 41–50. In measures 52–56 he lets strings 2 (C#) and 1 (E) ring out as the 3rd and 5th of A as he harmonizes notes from the A Mixolydian mode on string 3 underneath.

In a nod to both John Lee Hooker and Magic Sam, Winter implies chord changes in measures 23–41 for texture. Both the "Hook" and Sam usually only moved to the IV (D) chord, but, as you can see, Winter wanders far a field with C (♭III), F (♭VI), and G (♭VII) chord voicings. The result is intense musical tension that is released on beats 3–4 of measure 41 with the E/C# (5th/3rd) and A (root) functioning as the A major triad notes.

Winter comes sliding in (though not yet to "home") in measure 66 and continues bottlenecking on through to measure 83. Single notes from the A minor pentatonic scale, mostly on the upper strings at various fret positions, contrast with the B triad of D#/B/F# (3rd/root/5th) in measure 77, creating tension that is resolved to A in measure 78. In addition, a B dyad (D#/B) in measure 81 that is followed by a C dyad of G/C (5th/root) in measure 82 resolves quickly to A. Then, after having taken what almost amounts to a free-form solo (the album is called *The Progressive Blues Experiment*, after all!), Winter brings it all "back home" in measures 85–90 without the slide in the "interlude" similar to measures 7–12 of the verse, followed by Rhy. Fig. 1 in measures 91–95 in order to make a smooth, logical transition to verse 3 (not shown).

Performance Tip: Use your index finger like a slide to play the dyads in measures 23–41, being extra careful not to mute the open strings below.

Fig. 17

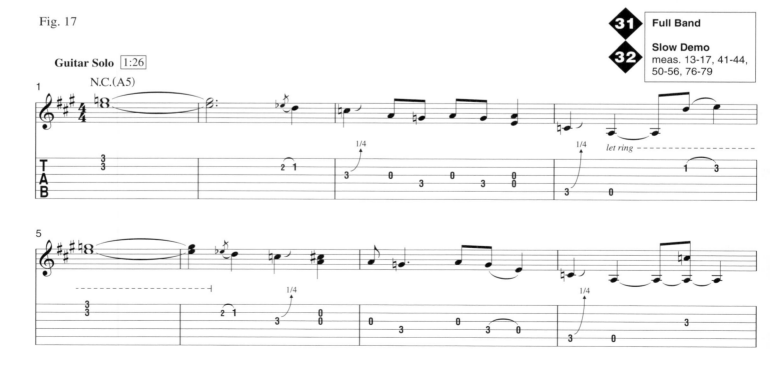

Guitar Solo 1:26

31 Full Band

32 Slow Demo
meas. 13-17, 41-44,
50-56, 76-79

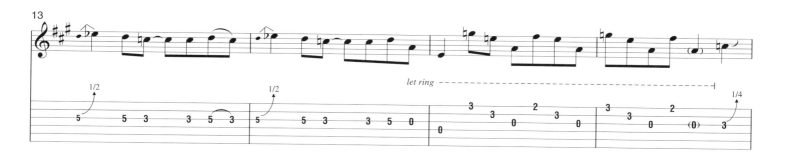

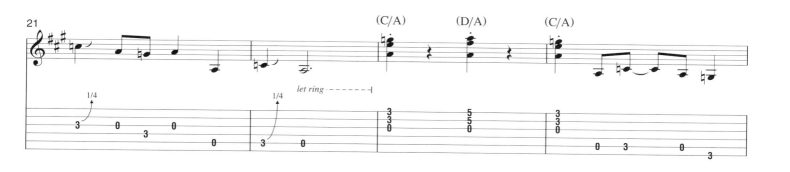

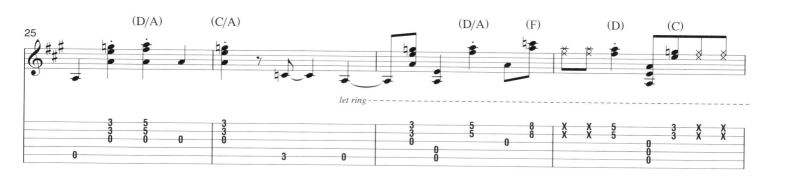

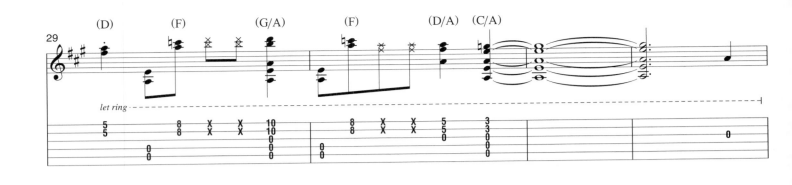

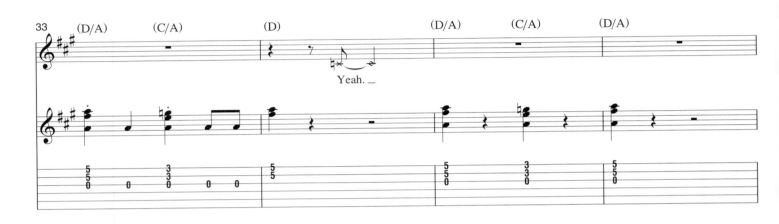

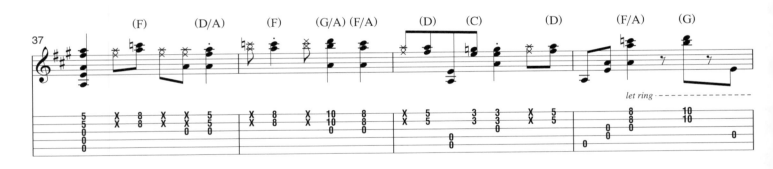

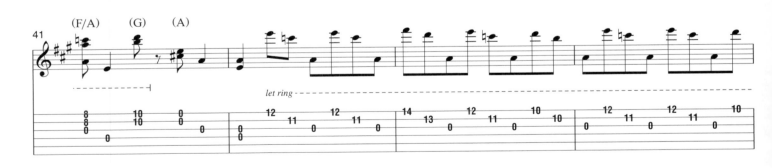

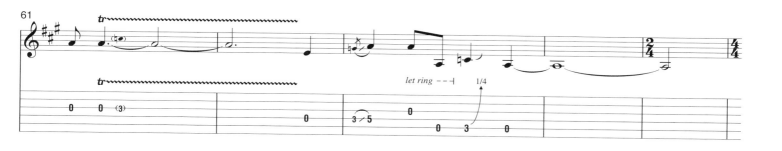

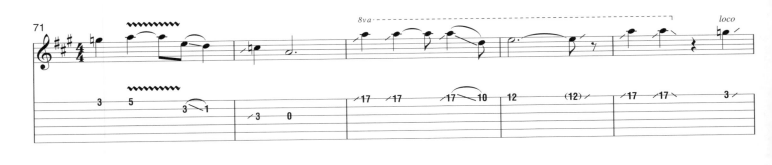

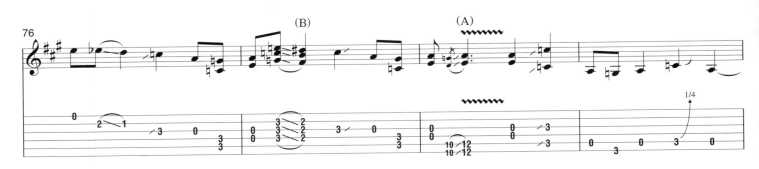

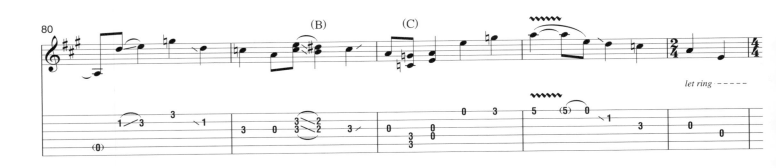

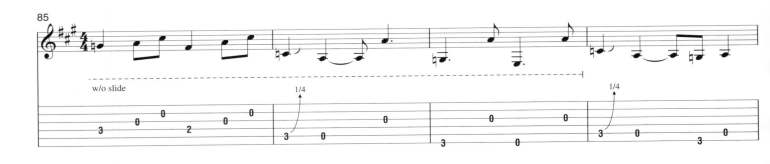

Gtr. 1: w/ Rhy. Fig. 1

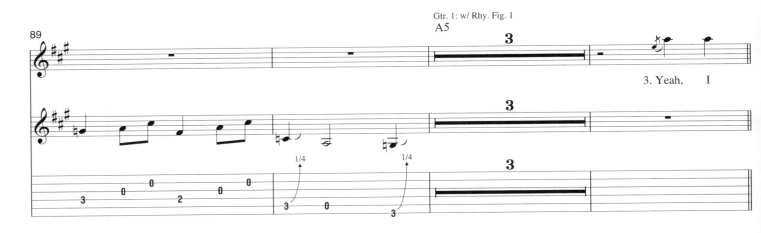

3. Yeah,   I

ROCK AND ROLL HOOCHIE KOO

(*Johnny Winter And,* 1970)
Words and Music by Rick Derringer

Guitarist Rick Derringer was only 17 years old in 1965 when he played a surprisingly credible blues rock solo on "Hang on Sloopy" with his band, the McCoys. By 1970 he had outgrown the teenybopper pop (though he would return to it to a degree in 1974 with his first solo album, *All American Boy*) when he and his brother Randy on drums were backing Johnny Winter. Derringer wrote "Rock and Roll Hoochie Koo" for Winter but, ironically, had the hit with it when he covered it on his solo debut. It has since gone on to become a staple of classic rock radio and innumerable bar bands.

Figure 18—Verse

Derringer got the glory, but Winter plays the way hotter guitar. The eight-measure progression (Rhy. Fig. 1) is built around a classic "call and response" format. A two-measure riff with one measure of A5 (I)–C5 (♭III)–D5 (IV) followed by a measure consisting of Winter (Gtr. 1) and Derringer (Gtr. 2) playing blues scale runs an octave apart (measures 2 and 6) or in harmony in 3rds and 4ths (measures 4 and 8). Observe how Winter and Derringer play complimentary rhythm parts with Winter using root position barre chord 5ths and Derringer employing 5ths with the 5th on the bottom for the A (A/E, except in measure 1 where he plays A/E/A), C (C/G), and D (D/A) changes. BTW: The "band called the Jokers" referenced in the lyrics was a real group featuring Dickey Betts.

Performance Tip: In measures 2 and 6 of Gtr. 1, bend the G (♭7th) up to A (root) with your pinky backed up by your ring, middle, and index fingers.

Fig. 18

1st Verse [0:15]

could-n't stop mov-in' when it first took hold,_____ it was a

Figure 19—Chorus

Almost identical to the intro (not shown) with two additional measures, the ten-measure chorus is one of the most memorable hooks in rock 'n' roll. Essentially it (Derringer as Gtr. 2) is constructed of two four-measure phrases of F (♭VI)–G (♭VII), A (I), F–G, and A. Note how the F and G changes are pumping boogie patterns while the A measures are embellished with quick C (♭III) and G changes for extra harmonic movement and interest. Measures 9–10 then resolve to an implied E7 (V) chord, like in a blues turnaround. Derringer completes his end of the bargain with the low E string struck open as he slides into D (♭7th) from C♯ on string 2.

Throughout the accompaniment of Gtr. 2, Winter (Gtr. 1) extends the harmony with triads, blues scale licks, and dyads. The effect is to bring out the "blues" in the blues rock composition. In measures 1 and 5 he pulls F/C, B♭/F, G/D, and C/E voicings out of his bag of tricks to layer additional harmony as well as incur more forward motion over Derringer's basic bass string boogie patterns. In measures 2–4 and 6–8 he keeps up a running musical commentary by offering seemingly spontaneous improvised licks along side triads and dyads tethered to specific chord changes. The former is brilliantly demonstrated in measure 2 where Winter creates tension by starting a run in the extension position ("Albert King box") of the A minor pentatonic scale, with an Albert King bend, and then descends to the root position where he resolves handsomely on the A note on beat 1 of measure 3 where it functions as the 3rd of F. Not finished yet, he plays C (5th) and D (6th) notes over the F5 and F6 changes before nailing the C and G changes with triads. For the capper, he bends the G (♭3rd) to the G♯ (3rd) in conjunction with the E (root) note in measures 9–10, producing a rich, vibrant E dominant tonality in combination with Derringer's licks.

Fig. 19

35 **Full Band**

36 **Slow Demo**
Gtr. 1   meas. 2-4, 6
Gtr. 2   meas. 2-3

Chorus 0:35

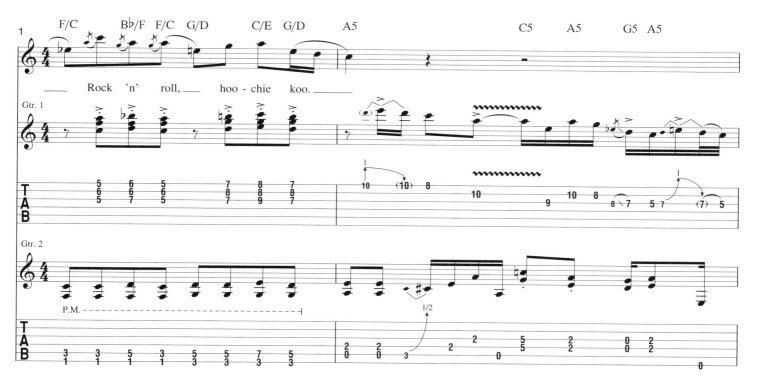

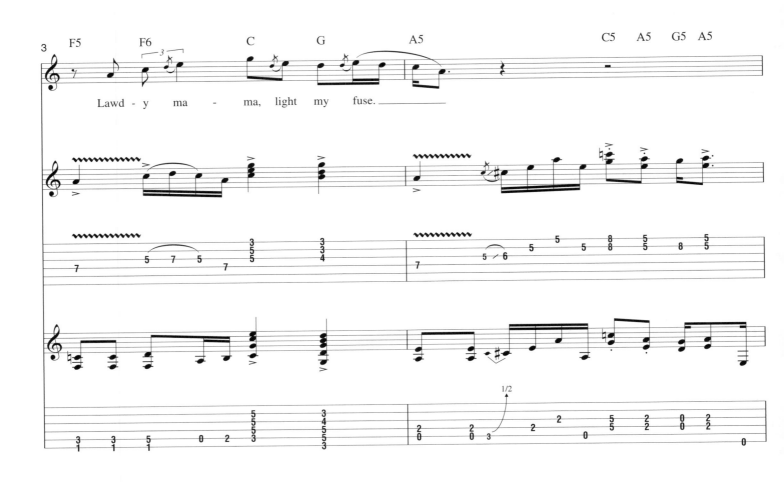

Lawd - y ma - ma, light my fuse. _____

Rock 'n' roll, _____ hoo - chie koo. _____

Truck on out _____ and spread ___ the news. _____

Al- right!

Figure 20—Guitar Solo

Winter (Gtr. 1) burns like a shorted hot plate in modal fashion over measure 1 from the verse functioning as Rhy. Fig. 1 (played by Gtr. 2), repeated eight times. Not surprisingly, he stays within the A blues scale, moving swiftly and fluidly between several positions for dynamic and dynamite musical tension. Dig his opening salvo with machine gun picking on the D (4th) bent one step to E (5th) and then gradually released before resolving to A (root) following C (♭3rd) on beat 3. The late, legendary Who drummer Keith Moon once quipped that, "...no one remembers the middle of your solo, only your entrance and exit." Now, that may be somewhat of a blanket statement, but it also contains more than a shred of truth. Lending power to his entrance with dynamic contrast, Winter immediately drops to the lower register in the root position of the scale before steadily ascending from the fifth position to the twelfth by measure 5.

Keeping the intensity level, as well as the frequency range at a peak, he rips through a repeating riff in measure 6 at fret 10 that most guitarists would likely play over a D (IV) chord rather than the A (I). Of course, it only adds to the musical tension that Winter begins to relax in measures 7–8 when he returns to the root position of the A blues scale at fret 5. Logically and satisfyingly, he runs down the scale with a whoosh to conclude his eight-measure rock 'n' roll romp by resolving to the A on beat 1 of verse 3 (not shown).

Performance Tip: In measure 6, barre strings 2 and 1 with your index finger and bend string 3 with your ring finger backed up by the middle.

Fig. 20

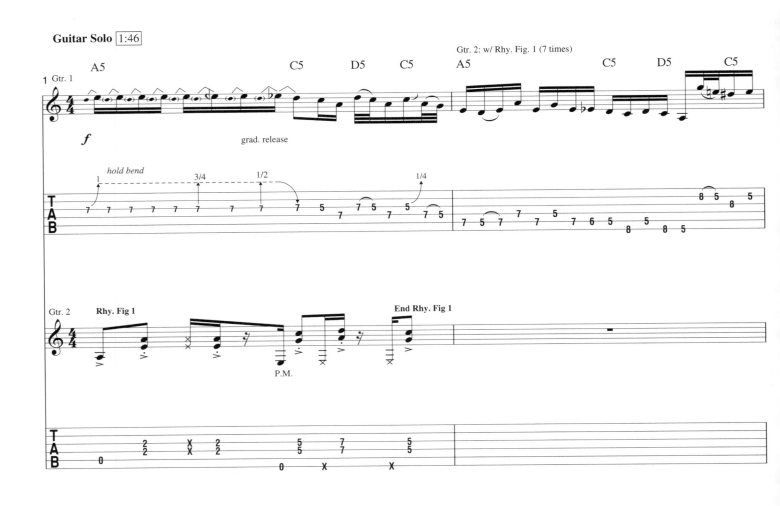

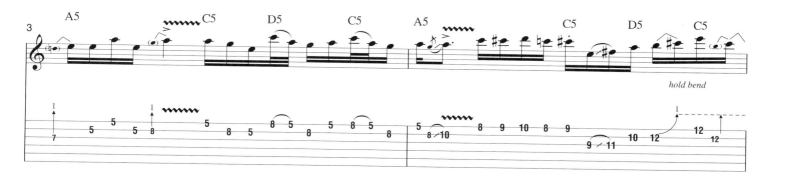

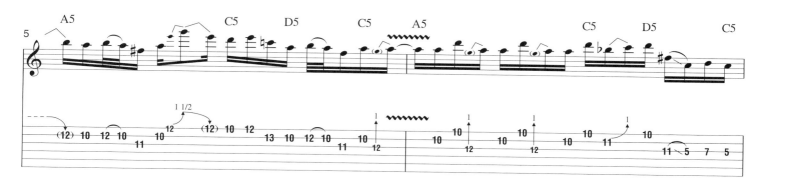

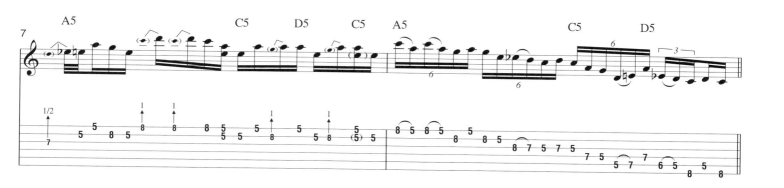

ROCK ME BABY
(*Still Alive and Well*, 1973)
Words and Music by B.B. King and Joe Bihan

As the opening track on his "comeback album," Johnny Winter takes "Rock Me Baby" up and out in a stunning, virtuosic display. As if it needed proving at this point, he confirms his status as one of the premier trio guitarists of all time, tossing off licks, solos, and boogie patterns in a torrent of notes not unlike a Texas flood!

Figure 21—Intro

The sixteen-measure intro is actually a 12-bar chorus with four extra measures of A5 (I) tacked on front where Winter plays unaccompanied. Combining flawless technique, perfect timing, and swinging phrasing, he accesses the open position and the root position box of the A blues scale at fret 5 for a rousing entrance. Observe his use of the open A (root) string to hold down the tonality and how his movement up the fingerboard constitutes a form of "call and response" with the open position. When the rhythm section enters in measure 5, Winter roams up and down through several positions of the scale while repeating bass string motifs in measures 11 and 16. Check out the "mandolin-strummed" dyads for creating musical tension in measures 7–8 where G/E ($\flat$7th/5th) at fret 15 implies an A7 tonality, and the way Winter follows the change to D5 (IV) in measures 9–10 by emphasizing the D (root) and C ($\flat$7th) notes. Also not to be missed in measure 13 is the hip bend over the E5 chord of F$\sharp$ (2nd) to G$\sharp$ (3rd) on string 2 against the B (5th) on string 1, nailing the E tonality.

Performance Tip: Bend the F$\sharp$ in measure 13 with your ring finger backed up by the middle and index, while holding the B with your pinky.

Fig. 21

*Chord symbols reflect implied harmony.

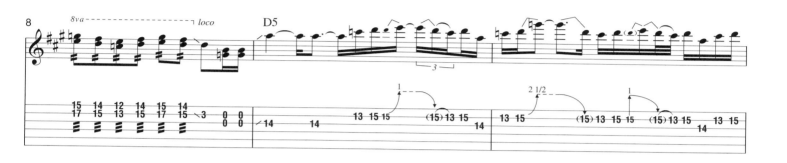

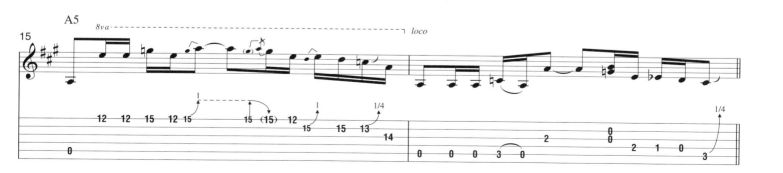

Figure 22—Verse

Winter rides the blues like a bucking bronco throughout the 12-bar verse via a variety of inventive means. Over the A5 (I) in measures 1–2 he mixes a modified, open string boogie pattern with a classic bend and pull-off in the root A minor pentatonic box at fret 5 within the span of one measure, followed by one of the most prominent bass string motifs from the intro in measure 3, and a "bendy" run in the root position box at fret 5 in measure 4. If this sounds like a lot of work, it is, but Winter makes it appear effortless. Slipping into his role as straight "rhythm man" in measures 6–7, Winter plays barred and open string D (IV) boogie patterns to give the momentum a substantial kick in the butt.

Perhaps it is by virtue of having to carry the main responsibility of clearly indicating the harmonic changes that compels Winter to eschew the modal playing for which he is rightly lionized. Nowhere is this more evident than in measure 9 over the E7 (V) chord where he literally strums a big, fat open position E7 voicing and then breaks it apart for extra rhythmic motion over beats 3–4. Also adding structure to the verse and the song in general is Winter's use of repeating motifs as in measures 7–8 over the A5 (I) change where he mimics the opening lick from measure 1 of the intro, one octave and then two octaves higher. In addition, in measure 10 over the D5 (IV) chord, he plays in unison with his vocal ("like my back ain't got no bone") for special emphasis as the bass and drums dynamically drop out.

Notice that the verse does not contain a turnaround in measures 11–12, but remains on the A5 (I) change instead in order to maintain forward momentum into the next twelve measures. Consequently, Winter keeps riffing in the A blues scale in the root and extension positions with musical tension generated by bends, especially the looping two-step one from the C ($\flat$3rd) to the E (5th) in measure 11, and resolution to the A (root) in both measures. Dig the blues-approved quarter-step bend to the "true blue note" between C and C# (3rd) on beat 4 of measure 12 that draws the listener to measure 1 of verse 2 (not shown).

Performance Tip: In measure 9, leave your index and pinky finger (low to high) in place on beat 3, and then quickly shift your index finger to the D note on string 2 at fret 3 following the open A string, hammering to the E at fret 5 with your ring finger.

41 Full Band

42 Slow Demo
Gtr. 1 meas. 9-12

Fig. 22

Figure 23—Guitar Solo

Winter rocks his "baby" and everyone else through two, jalapeno pepper-powered 12-bar choruses. As he is often wont to do, he makes a grand entrance in measures 1–3 of the first chorus with mandolin-strummed triple stops implying A7 tonality (C♯/G/E = 3rd/♭7th/5th) contrasted with C major triads (E/C/G = 3rd/root/5th) as substitutes supplying musical tension. In measure 4 he segues into G/E (♭7th/5th) dyads to further extend the A7 tonality before launching into a firestorm of mostly single-note lines. As a trio guitarist playing over the bass, it is imperative that he mark the changes at least occasionally during his basically modal outing. Measure 5 over the D5 (IV) is indicative of that approach as Winter makes sure to emphasize the D (root) note at fret 15 on string 2. In measure 7 over the A5 (I) chord, he eases into the fourteenth position of the A major pentatonic scale, also known colloquially as the F♯ relative minor pentatonic scale, to lay into the A (root) and C♯ (3rd) notes to acknowledge the change. The E5 (V) change in measure 9 is implied with emphasis on the E (root) note in the root position of the A blues scale with patented Winter sextuplets as he makes a subtle shift in emphasis from the root (A) note of the A5 (I) chord in the same scale position in measure 8. Do not miss the dynamic rest of the rhythm section in measure 10, where he executes a woozy, time-stopping double-string bend of D/A (root/5th) to define the tonality. Capping his first solo chorus is a tangy C/A (♭3rd/root) dyad in measure 12 over the A5 (I) chord.

In the second chorus Winter takes a slightly different tack, playing somewhat fewer notes and giving more attention to navigating the harmonic changes. In measures 13–14, he makes a passing reference to the C♯/G/E (3rd/♭7th/5th) triple-stop that led off the first chorus before ripping into a spectacular one and one-half step series of bends of E (5th) to G (♭7th) in measure 16. D (root) notes in varying locations abound in measures 17–18 over the D5 (IV) change, including string 4 (D) open, as do A (5th) notes to firm up the tonality. A bracing dynamic shift occurs in measure 19 over the A5 (I) chord when Winter drops into the lower register on the bass strings as a figurative "recharging of his batteries" with string 5 (A) open and G/A (♭7th/root) coolly accessed with the fretted G and string 5 open. Measure 20 shows harmonic adventureness over the tonic chord not usually observed in the playing of "Johnny Guitar" as he follows G/E (♭7th/5th) with E/C/G (5th/♭3rd/♭7th) that would read as a C/E first inversion triad over a C chord change. The effect in this context, however, is one of hip A tonality blues harmony, even if only briefly. Pugnacious bends from the D (♭7th) to the E (root) in measure 21 over the E5 (V) change at the fifteenth position set up the stop-time in measure 22 over the D5 (IV) chord where Winter relocates to the root octave position of the A minor pentatonic scale at the seventeenth position for a searing bend of the C (♭7th) to the E♭ (♭9th) for maximum musical tension. The climax of his solo is reached in the penultimate measure 23 over the A (I) chord where he lays out an explosive lick of the A (root), G (♭7th), and D bent to E (5th) in the same position for surprising resolution implying an A7 voicing that is reinforced with root, 5th, and ♭7th notes in measure 24.

Performance Tip: For the lick in measure 23, try this fingering, high to low: index, pinky, and ring (backed up by the middle finger) for the bend.

Fig. 23

43 Full Band

44 Slow Demo
Gtr. 1 meas. 4-10,
14-16, 21-24

Guitar Solo 2:10

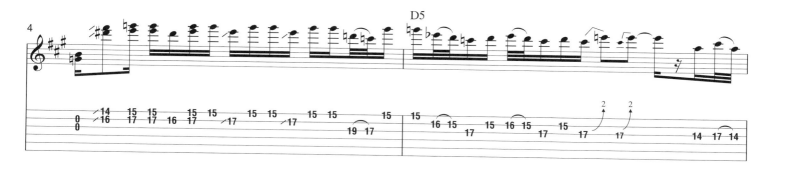

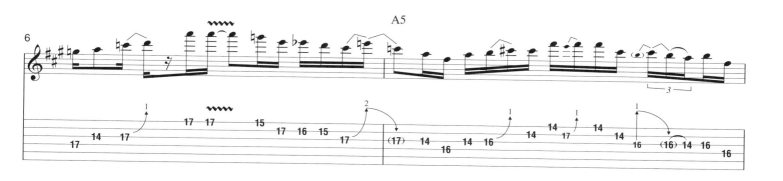

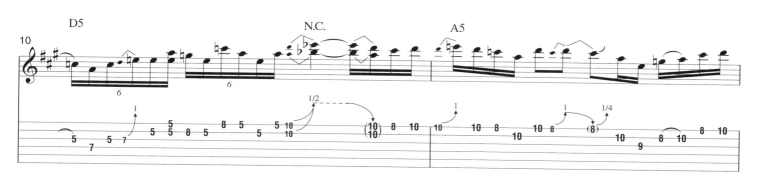

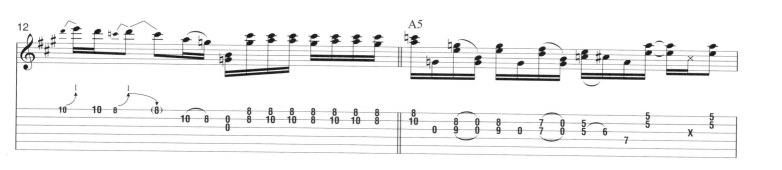

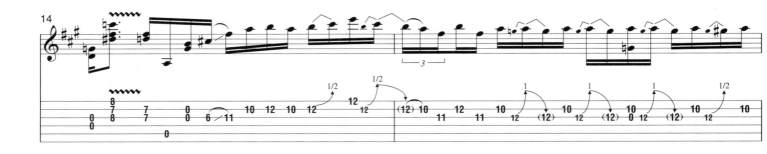

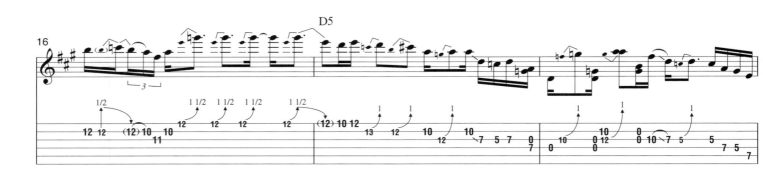

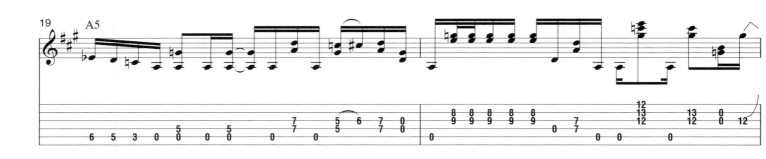

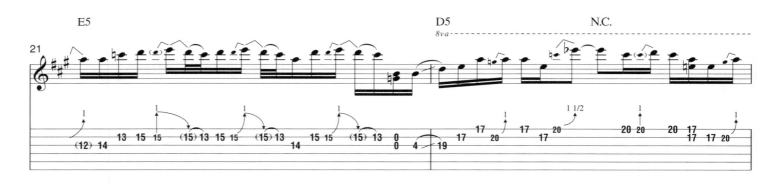

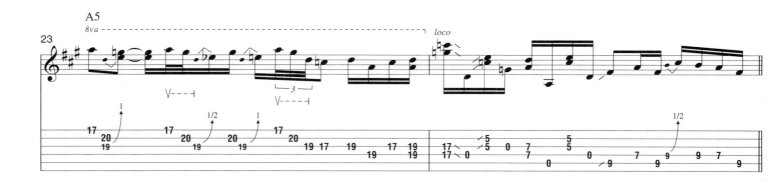

STILL ALIVE AND WELL
(*Still Alive and Well*, 1973)
Words and Music by Rick Derringer

Besides the Rolling Stones, who Johnny Winter covers better than any one else, Rick Derringer proved to be a fine source of material. Along with the rambunctious, blues- rocking funk of the title track, the real "McCoy" also contributed "Cheap Tequila" to his buddy's triumphant comeback album.

Figure 24—Verse

Measures 1–4 of the eight-measure verse contain a classic "call and response" with Winter literally singing the "call" in measures 1 and 3 and "responding" with his loquacious axe in measures 2 and 4. Complimenting the wry lyrics is a riff in measure 2, repeated exactly in measure 4, which rushes forward with both terrific power and fluidity in the root position of the A minor pentatonic scale. Dig how G (5th) to C (root) and D (5th) to G (root) imply C and G changes on beats 3 and 4, respectively. Also observe how ending the riff on the G (♭7th) "leads" the ear back to the A (root) note in measure 3 and down to the open E (root) string in measure 5 courtesy of the descending bass line. Starting in measure 5 the progression advances upward with accelerating momentum through E (V), F♯m (vi), G (♭VII), D5 (IV), and E5 chord changes as Winter approaches each change with either a different voicing and/or fill. Simple bass-string major triads and double stops phrased with syncopation suffice for the E. Minor triads blended with cool, Hendrix-like melodic fills from the root position of the F♯ minor pentatonic scale illuminate the F♯m change, an octave dynamically outlines the G harmony, while the D5 and E5 changes only need power chords to make the rapid transition to the chorus.

Performance Tip: Access the double-string bends of F♯/D (6th/4th) in measures 1 and 4 with your ring and pinky fingers, low to high.

Fig. 24

45 Full Band

46 Slow Demo
meas. 2 (w/pickup), 6

* Chord symbols reflect implied harmony.

Figure 25—Chorus

Winter "tears the roof off the sucka" in the chorus with eight measures of back-snapping funk rhythm guitar. Notice that the progression is composed of two four-measure phrases of A (I), D (IV), E (V), and D5–C5 (♭III)–A5 that build upward in intensity and then cycle back to the I chord. Where a lesser player may have repeated the same forms and voicings twice, Winter cleverly employs basic open position chords in measures 1–3 with power chords and a bluesy run in the root position of the A minor pentatonic scale in measure 4. In measures 5–7, however, he plays a classic blues riff used to nail the major tonality for each change in a parallel fashion. Dripping with fatback grease and exceptionally suited to funky, syncopated strumming, it drives the chord progression forward with unrelenting momentum. Measure 8 is similar to measure 4 for the D5 and C5 changes, but Winter opts to dip into the A major pentatonic scale at the second position on beats 3–4, providing a more satisfying resolution to the A (I) tonality as it ends on A/E (root/5th).

Performance Tip: For the hip riffs in measures 5–7, barre with your index finger at frets 5, 10, and 12, hammering to the appropriate major 3rd (C♯, F♯, or G♯ at frets 6, 11, and 13, respectively) with your middle finger. Play the implied IV chord change at frets 7, 12, and 14 with your ring finger as a small barre.

Fig. 25 0:38

Chorus

still a-live__ and well,____ I'm still a-live__ and well,____

Gtr. 1

Ev-'ry now and then I know it's kind a hard to tell, but I'm still a-live__ and well.__

Still a-live__ and well,____ still a-live__ and well.____

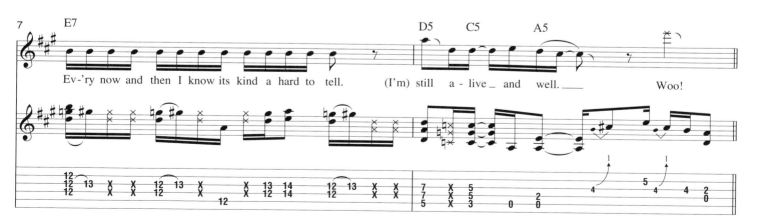

Ev-'ry now and then I know its kind a hard to tell. (I'm) still a-live__ and well.____ Woo!

Figure 26—Guitar Solo

The four measures of E (V) from the interlude (not shown), the eight-measure verse, and the eight-measure chorus are creatively combined to form a dynamic twenty-measure progression that Winter rides over with glee. Having the E make an appearance right out of the gate automatically produces musical tension as Winter wails in the root octave position of the E minor pentatonic scale at fret 12 before galloping his way down through the fifth and open positions. As opposed to his usual modal calling card, in measure 3 he adds rich harmony and melody over the churning, angular rhythms. Here he plays through the changes with the appropriate matching scale.

Measures 5–12 are the adrenalin-pumping dynamic center of the solo and contain four two-measure increments consisting of a measure of stop-time over A5 (I) and a measure of A–C5 (♭III)–G5 (♭VII) that is similar to measures 2–4 of the verse. The "response" in measures 6, 8, 10, and 12 of A5 (I)–C5 (♭III)–G5 (♭VII) is virtually the same with a stinging run down the root position of the A minor pentatonic scale. Be sure to check out the blues-approved dyad of C/E (♭3rd/5th) at fret 5. Also, do not miss the unusual triple stop with a bend in measure 13 over the A5 (I) that produces C/G/G (♭3rd/♭7th/♭7th) to create smoldering blues tension. With his sights set on the finish line in measure 20, however, Winter begins in measure 14 with scale and note choices reflecting each chord change, and in the process presents resolution as well. Over the D5 (IV) and E5 (V) changes in measures 14 and 15, respectively, he literally relocates to the root position of the D and E composite scales (blues scale combined with Mixolydian mode) and is careful to include the major 3rds (F♯ and G♯) and ♭7ths (C and D) to imply a bluesy D7 and E7 tonality.

In measures 16–20 (save for measure 18, where he resorts back to the D composite scale) Winter employs several positions of the A minor pentatonic scale with consummate skill as he fluidly brings his raucous solo to a satisfying conclusion without a dip in the energy department. Dig how he mimics the melody line of "still alive and well" in measure 16 over D5–C5–A5 and then alludes to it again in measure 20 over the same changes.

Performance Tip: In measure 9 be sure to use alternate down and up pick strokes to play the hip ascending line. Check out how Jimmy Page also used it on occasion, most notably in its descending form in the coda of "Good Times, Bad Times."

Fig. 26

Guitar Solo [1:51]

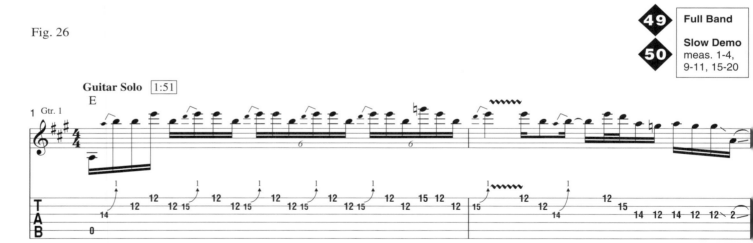

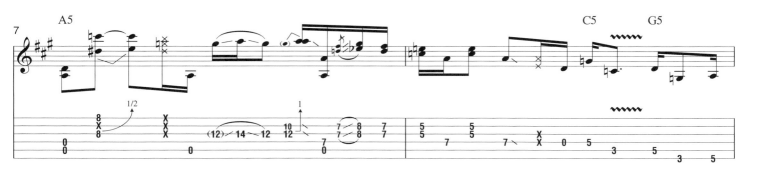

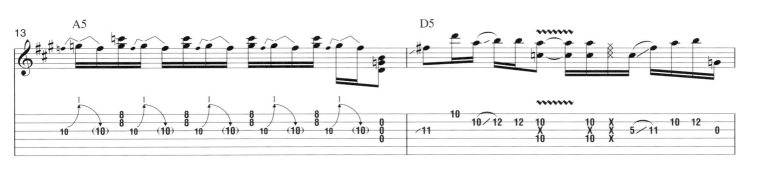

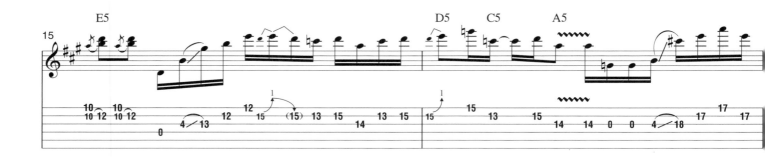

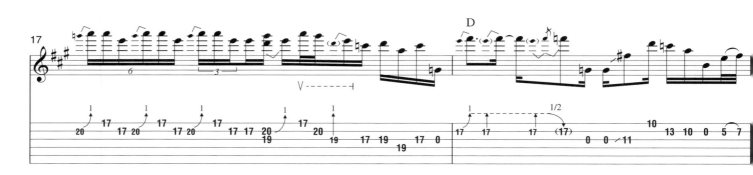

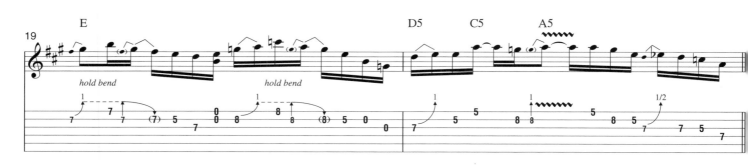

SWEET LOVE & EVIL WOMEN

(*Nothin' But The Blues*, 1977)
Written by Johnny Winter

Though Johnny Winter's mentor and "father," Muddy Waters, did not cotton to open D tuning as much as open G, "Sweet Love & Evil Women" is yet another nod in his direction by virtue of the slide guitar phrasing. "Chicago," meet "Texas."

Figure 27—Verse

Note: Gtr. 1 (Winter) is tuned to open D, while Gtr. 2 ("Steady Rollin'" Bob Margolin) is tuned one whole step down to facilitate playing in the key of D while thinking in the key of E.

The 12-bar verse contains the "fast IV change" to the G7 (IV) chord in measure 2. Citing a time-honored tradition, Winter (Gtr. 1) fingers a D7 voicing of F#/C/A (3rd/♭7th/5th) in measure 1 and then lowers the pattern one fret in measure 2 to what could be considered D♭7, but is instead a hip G7♭9 voicing of F/B/G# (♭7th/3rd/ ♭9th) in this context. Amazingly, throughout the next ten measures and in all of the verses not shown, he plays slide fills and licks while simultaneously singing; not just "call and response," he literally plays counter melodies while vocalizing. If this is any proof, his late guitar buddy Jimi Hendrix had nothing on him in this regard! For instance, dig the way he follows the changes with D/A (root/5th) in measure 3 over the D7 (I) chord and the notes D (5th) and B (3rd) in measures 5–6 of the G7 (IV) chord. By contrast, in measures 7–8 over the D7 chord he drops to the lower register and honks on the A (5th), F# (3rd), and C (♭7th) notes for swirling, blues-drenched licks.

Performance Tip: As always when playing slide, wear your slide on your pinky so you can easily finger the chords in measures 1–2 with your index, middle, and ring fingers.

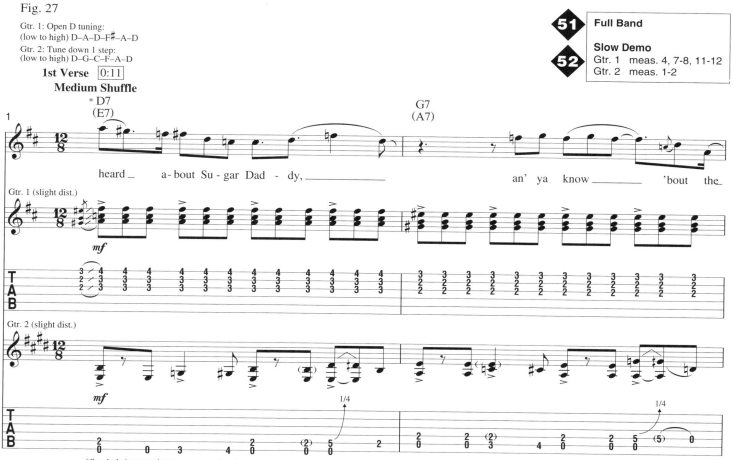

Fig. 27

Gtr. 1: Open D tuning:
(low to high) D–A–D–F#–A–D
Gtr. 2: Tune down 1 step:
(low to high) D–G–C–F–A–D

51 Full Band

52 Slow Demo
Gtr. 1 meas. 4, 7-8, 11-12
Gtr. 2 meas. 1-2

1st Verse 0:11

Medium Shuffle

heard __ a-bout Su-gar Dad - dy, _____ an' ya know _____ 'bout the_

*Symbols in parentheses represent chord names respective to detuned guitar.
Symbols above reflect actual sounding chords.

Published by WINTER BLUES MUSIC (BMI)

Figure 28—Guitar Solo

Winter (Gtr. 1) sounds as though he is having way too much fun playing the Chicago blues slide guitar he so reveres. In this case, Chicago blues not only means Muddy Waters, but Elmore James as well as he wiggles his slider at regular intervals similarly to James' epochal "Dust My Broom" motif. Two twelve-measure choruses with the "slow IV change" affords him the acreage to subtly navigate the changes with style and confidence born of the many years of deep study to which he dedicated the earlier part of his life.

When he is not at the root octave position of open D tuning at fret 12 (like Elmore), as in measures 7–8 over the D (I) chord, Winter favors creating musical tension at fret 3 in measures 1–2 and 11 with emphasis on the C (♭7th) on string 2. He then resolves with regularity to strings 2 (A) and 1 (D) open. Check out how he applies the same concept to measure 5 over the G (IV) chord with the F (♭7th) emphasized at fret 3 on string 1. Nailing choice "target notes" like the ♭7th is a shrewd way to help define chord changes when not literally changing keys with each change. In measure 6 over the G chord, Winter moves up to fret 10 and grinds on the A(9th) and C(4th) notes, heightening the tension in anticipation of the D chord to come in measures 7–8.

Winter approaches measures 13–16 over the D (I) change in the second chorus with similar licks as in the first chorus, though he whips up to the root octave position in measure 14 as a way of tightening up the tension and as a form of "call and response." In measures 17–18 over the G (IV) chord, though, he decides to become more specific with his note selection and slides over F (♭7th), G (root), and G♯ (♭2nd as a passing tone) on the way to A (2nd) in measure 18 that resolves to G on the second half of beat 4 with very vocal-like phrasing. Working the spicy tension engendered around fret 3 in conjunction with the open strings is an effective dynamic in measures 19–20 over the D (I) chord that sets up the inflammatory climax of the solo in measures 21–22 over the A (V) and G (IV) changes that follow. Observe how the root octave position in measure 21 echoes that of measure 14 and that the F♯ and A notes on strings 3 and 2 function as the melodic 6th and root of the A chord. Taking it almost to the limit in measure 22, Winter climbs higher to fret 15 where the A and C notes become the dominant 9th and tension-inducing sus4 of the G chord. Using the dynamics of register as well as note selection and phrasing to drive home his musical statement, Winter returns to his motif of utilizing fret 3 and the open strings in measure 23, and in measure 24 over the A chord where A and C on strings 3 and 2 function as the root and ♭3rd "blues note."

Performance Tip: Though a minor detail, do not miss the fretted passage on beat 4 of measure 18 in chorus 2 that should be played with your index and ring fingers (hence, the reason for wearing your slider on your pinky finger).

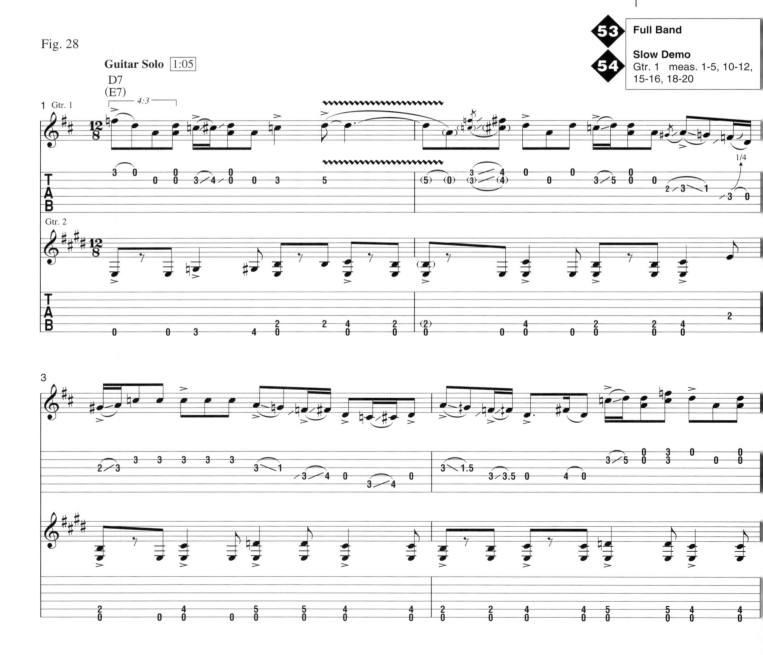

Fig. 28

Figure 29—Outro Solo

As befits the ultimate climax of the tune, Winter (Gtr. 1) spends the bulk of his time in the last twelve measures at frets 15, 17, 19, 21, and 24! Have mercy! Dig that in this breath-taking ascension in measures 1–6 he is thinking of creating (or maybe just "feeling") tremendous musical anticipation via the effect of moving up so high on the neck, as opposed to the function of each pitch. That said, he brilliantly ends up on the B (3rd) and D (5th) notes of G at frets 21 and 24, respectively, in measures 5 and 6, for resolution, before dropping off dynamically to the lower register through to the end of his solo and the song. Observe with wonder how Winter also does his slippin' and slidin' below fret 3 while managing to indicate, at least tangentially, each chord change. Of particular interest is measure 9 (A), where he nips the G (♭7th), C♯ (3rd), and root (A) notes, and measure 10 (G) with the F (♭7th) and D (5th) notes. Exhibiting a touch of anarchy on beats 6–12 over measure 12 (D), he sustains C/A (♭7th/5th) for a dollop of dominant harmony rather than prosaically stopping and simply resolving to D (root). Bravo, Johnny Guitar!

Performance Tip: Keep your vibrato in a tight, controlled shimmy in measure 4 in order to precisely focus on the ascending pitches.

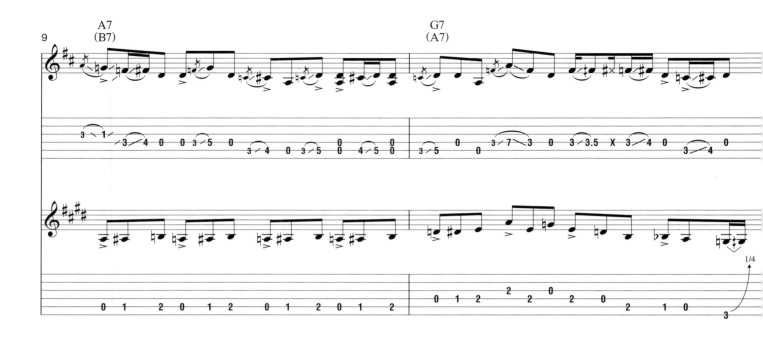

TV MAMA
(*Nothin' But the Blues*, 1977)
Written by Johnny Winter

Fittingly, the last song in the book has Johnny Winter performing solo on the National Steel with his own bass drum accompaniment. Not coincidentally, Muddy Waters similarly recorded "She Moves Me" in 1951 with the master Little Walter blowing harp and Chess Records president Leonard Chess playing the big bass drum.

Note that Winter employs the slide-approved tuning of open G, but a capo on fret 3 causes the song to sound in the key of B♭. To avoid confusion, Roman numerals and scale degree numbers are used exclusively in the analysis instead of pitch names.

Figure 30—Verse 1

Winter cites the legendary Robert Johnson, who also influenced Muddy Waters, as one of his main guys. His twelve-measure blues "TV Mama" with the "slow IV change" bears a striking musical resemblance to both Johnson's "Terraplane Blues" and "Crossroads Blues," and a lyrical association to the former number as regards to the leering imagery.

Be aware that Winter switches from fretted to slide licks throughout, as can be readily seen and heard in measures 1–4 over the I chord. Note how the fretted dominant triple stop of ♭7th/5th/root, forming an implied I7, could not be accessed with the slide, as string 3 must be open. The same concept is accomplished in measure 9 over the V chord, where Winter fingers root/♭7th/4th to imply a funky V7 voicing. Again, know that strings 3 and 1 are struck open.

In measures 5–6 over the IV, he literally relocates to fret 5 where the IV triad (spread out over all six strings) resides in a classic country blues guitar move prized by bottleneckers playing in open tunings. Be aware that a parallel move up the fingerboard to fret 7 would produce the V chord, though Winter chooses not to do so in "TV Mama."

Performance Tip: Both the I7 and V chords in measures 1–2 and 9, respectively, may be played with just the index finger.

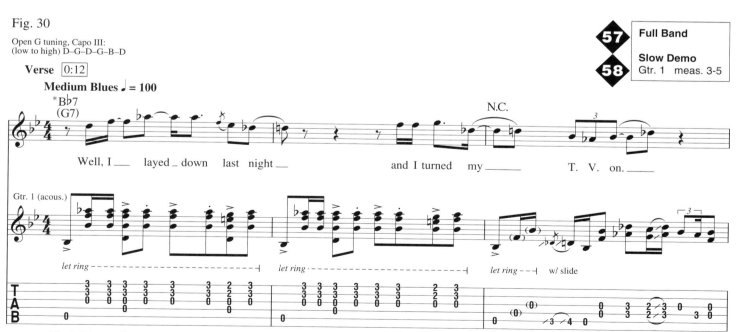

Fig. 30

Open G tuning, Capo III:
(low to high) D–G–D–G–B–D

Verse [0:12]

57 — Full Band

58 — Slow Demo / Gtr. 1 meas. 3-5

Medium Blues ♩ = 100

*Symbols in parentheses represent chord names respective to capoed guitar.
Symbols above reflect actual sounding chords. Capoed fret is "0" in tab.

*gradually increase rate and depth of vibrato.

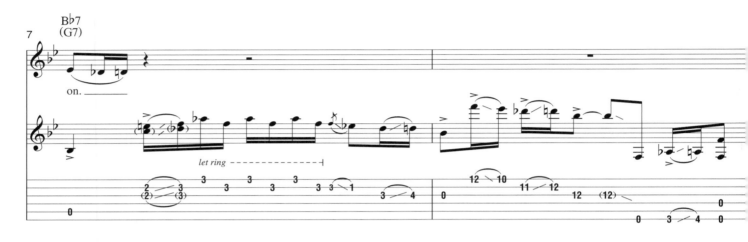

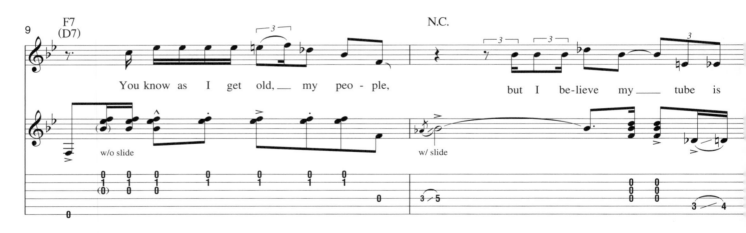

Figure 31—Verse 3

In verse 3 Winter makes the hippest shift from the stomping "flat four" rhythm that drives the majority of the tune, to a shuffle in measures 1–3. Appropriately enough, he also employs fretted walking bass lines as his harmonic underpinning in a sly nod to both Johnson and Waters. Further mimicking Johnson, with all due respect, he offers a fingered pattern in measure 5 over the IV chord reminiscent of RJ's version of "Walking Blues" before resorting to the slide at fret 5 for the IV triad in measure 6 as in verse 1.

In measures 7–8 over the I chord, Winter applies his innate sense of dynamics by creating tension with the slide at fret 3 with the 5th and ♭7th notes before zooming up to the root octave position at fret 12 for the 5th, 4th, ♭3rd as a grace note, 3rd, and root. Notice how strings 3 and 5 are picked open so as to leave no doubt as to the tonality being proffered. Particular attention should also be paid to measures 11–12 (that remain on the I, as in all verses, rather than move to V in measure 12 as a "turn around" back to the I chord), where Winter shows off his precision with a nifty run down the root position of the tonic minor pentatonic scale. Check out how Winter glisses into almost every note from one fret above or below, an important characteristic of slide guitar playing that should be incorporated repeatedly.

Performance Tip: The Robert Johnson-type lick in measure 5 will have to be executed with the index (fret 5) and ring (fret 8) fingers.

Fig. 31

Figure 32—Guitar Solo

Winter gets his jollies careening through two 12-bar choruses of blues, with one surprising exception: The second chorus contains thirteen measures as he tacks on an extra measure of the I chord following measure 12. Likely, he was having so much fun he just could not help himself. At any rate, he certainly plays his solo with gusto, in the process providing a course in advanced slide guitar. In measure 4 over the I change in the first chorus, he leans hard on the ♭7th to "lead" the ear to the IV chord in measures 5–6. However, rather than resolving to the IV in measure 5 after creating musical tension in measure 4, he starts off with the ♭7th note an octave lower, where it functions as the tart sus4th of the IV chord. Not to worry, however, as Winter does resolve with clarity in measure 6 via the IV major triad at fret 5. Be aware that he tends to emphasize the lower register in the first chorus as a set-up for the more climactic, high-register riffing in the second chorus. This approach is particularly effective in measures 8, 9, and 10, where dyads on strings 5 and 4 add harmonic substance along with gravelly bass tones. Dig that the dyads and phrasing in measure 9 are a direct tribute to the Muddy Waters style as found in, among others, "I Can't Be Satisfied" from 1948.

The second chorus commences with a flash as Winter wiggles around at fret 12. In measure 14, he manufactures wobbly tension by moving down chromatically on strings 2 and 1 to frets 11 and 10 and then returning to fret 12 in measure 15. Capping the four measures of I is a fingered I7 voicing of root/♭7th/root in measure 16 spiced with root/6th that makes for an alternating I7–I6 pattern. On a roll, Winter walks up string 5 in measures 17–18 over the IV starting with the open fifth string and ascends chromatically. Measure 20 contains a welcome dollop of fingered harmony with root/♭5th/root, ♭7th/5th/root/5th, and root/5th/root/5th in anticipation of the V chord that follows in measure 21. Observe how Winter uses ascending bass string patterns in measures 21 and 22 as motifs in the spirit of measures 17–18 and how they help propel the solo forward. Likewise, the "bonus" measure of the I chord in measure 25 repeats a similar pattern of fretted voicings as found in measure 20. How apropos for Winter to end his solo like the originators from the 1920s and 1930s who cared not a whit about regular beats and measures, but whatever helped them to put across their feelings for the blues.

Performance Tip: For beats 1-2 in measure 20 of the second chorus, anchor your ring finger at fret 5 on string 1 (a stretch!). Play frets 2 and 3 on string 2 with your index finger, but barre fret 3 with your index finger for beat 2. Additionally, utilize your index finger for the barred dyads on beats 3–4.

Fig. 32

61 Full Band

62 Slow Demo
Gtr. 1 meas. 3-4,
7-10, 17-20

Guitar Solo 1:34

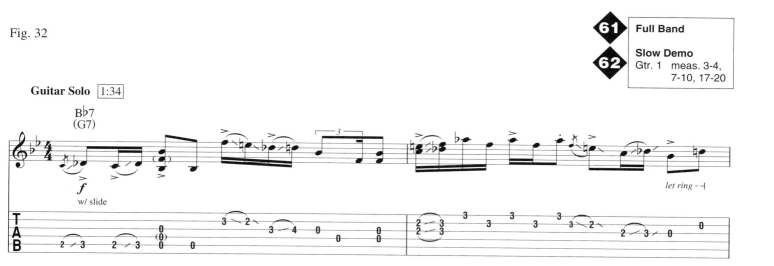

91

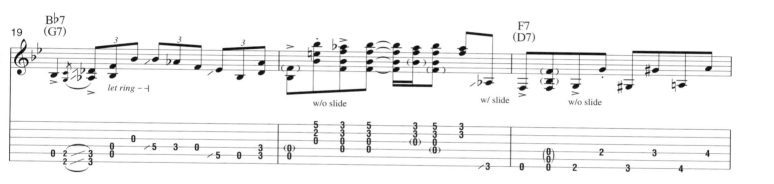

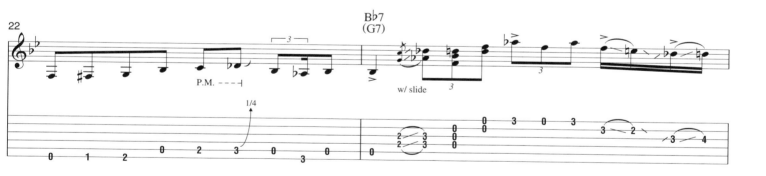

Guitar Notation Legend

Guitar Music can be notated three different ways: on a *musical staff*, in *tablature*, and in *rhythm slashes*.

RHYTHM SLASHES are written above the staff. Strum chords in the rhythm indicated. Use the chord diagrams found at the top of the first page of the transcription for the appropriate chord voicings. Round noteheads indicate single notes.

THE MUSICAL STAFF shows pitches and rhythms and is divided by bar lines into measures. Pitches are named after the first seven letters of the alphabet.

TABLATURE graphically represents the guitar fingerboard. Each horizontal line represents a a string, and each number represents a fret.

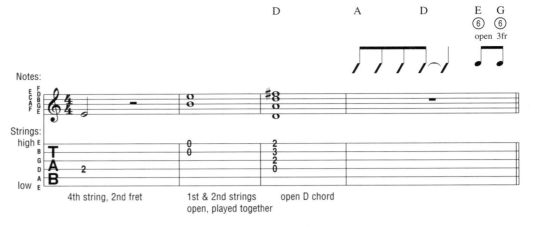

4th string, 2nd fret

1st & 2nd strings open, played together

open D chord

Definitions for Special Guitar Notation

HALF-STEP BEND: Strike the note and bend up 1/2 step.

WHOLE-STEP BEND: Strike the note and bend up one step.

GRACE NOTE BEND: Strike the note and immediately bend up as indicated.

SLIGHT (MICROTONE) BEND: Strike the note and bend up 1/4 step.

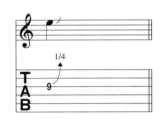

BEND AND RELEASE: Strike the note and bend up as indicated, then release back to the original note. Only the first note is struck.

PRE-BEND: Bend the note as indicated, then strike it.

PRE-BEND AND RELEASE: Bend the note as indicated. Strike it and release the bend back to the original note.

UNISON BEND: Strike the two notes simultaneously and bend the lower note up to the pitch of the higher.

VIBRATO: The string is vibrated by rapidly bending and releasing the note with the fretting hand.

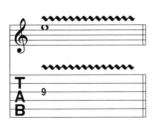

WIDE VIBRATO: The pitch is varied to a greater degree by vibrating with the fretting hand.

HAMMER-ON: Strike the first (lower) note with one finger, then sound the higher note (on the same string) with another finger by fretting it without picking.

PULL-OFF: Place both fingers on the notes to be sounded. Strike the first note and without picking, pull the finger off to sound the second (lower) note.

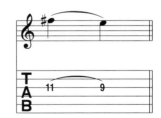

LEGATO SLIDE: Strike the first note and then slide the same fret-hand finger up or down to the second note. The second note is not struck.

SHIFT SLIDE: Same as legato slide, except the second note is struck.

TRILL: Very rapidly alternate between the notes indicated by continuously hammering on and pulling off.

TAPPING: Hammer ("tap") the fret indicated with the pick-hand index or middle finger and pull off to the note fretted by the fret hand.

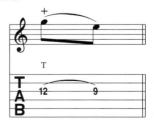

NATURAL HARMONIC: Strike the note while the fret-hand lightly touches the string directly over the fret indicated.

PINCH HARMONIC: The note is fretted normally and a harmonic is produced by adding the edge of the thumb or the tip of the index finger of the pick hand to the normal pick attack.

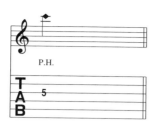

HARP HARMONIC: The note is fretted normally and a harmonic is produced by gently resting the pick hand's index finger directly above the indicated fret (in parentheses) while the pick hand's thumb or pick assists by plucking the appropriate string.

PICK SCRAPE: The edge of the pick is rubbed down (or up) the string, producing a scratchy sound.

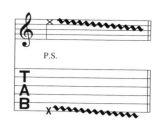

MUFFLED STRINGS: A percussive sound is produced by laying the fret hand across the string(s) without depressing, and striking them with the pick hand.

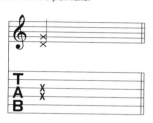

PALM MUTING: The note is partially muted by the pick hand lightly touching the string(s) just before the bridge.

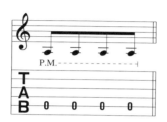

RAKE: Drag the pick across the strings indicated with a single motion.

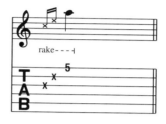

TREMOLO PICKING: The note is picked as rapidly and continuously as possible.

ARPEGGIATE: Play the notes of the chord indicated by quickly rolling them from bottom to top.

VIBRATO BAR DIVE AND RETURN: The pitch of the note or chord is dropped a specified number of steps (in rhythm) then returned to the original pitch.

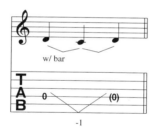

VIBRATO BAR SCOOP: Depress the bar just before striking the note, then quickly release the bar.

VIBRATO BAR DIP: Strike the note and then immediately drop a specified number of steps, then release back to the original pitch.

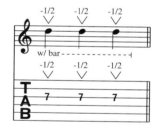

Additional Musical Definitions

 (accent)
- Accentuate note (play it louder)

 (accent)
- Accentuate note with great intensity

 (staccato)
- Play the note short

- Downstroke

∨
- Upstroke

D.S. al Coda
- Go back to the sign (𝄋), then play until the measure marked "*To Coda*," then skip to the section labelled "**Coda**."

D.C. al Fine
- Go back to the beginning of the song and play until the measure marked "*Fine*" (end).

Rhy. Fig.
- Label used to recall a recurring accompaniment pattern (usually chordal).

Riff
- Label used to recall composed, melodic lines (usually single notes) which recur.

Fill
- Label used to identify a brief melodic figure which is to be inserted into the arrangement.

Rhy. Fill
- A chordal version of a Fill.

tacet
- Instrument is silent (drops out).

- Repeat measures between signs.

- When a repeated section has different endings, play the first ending only the first time and the second ending only the second time.

NOTE: Tablature numbers in parentheses mean:
1. The note is being sustained over a system (note in standard notation is tied), or
2. The note is sustained, but a new articulation (such as a hammer-on, pull-off, slide or vibrato begins), or
3. The note is a barely audible "ghost" note (note in standard notation is also in parentheses).

GUITAR *signature licks*®

Signature Licks book/CD packs provide a step-by-step breakdown of "right from the record" riffs, licks, and solos so you can jam along with your favorite bands. They contain performance notes and an overview of each artist's or group's style, with note-for-note transcriptions in notes and tab. The CDs feature full-band demos at both normal and slow speeds.

ACOUSTIC CLASSICS
00695864 ....$19.95

BEST OF ACOUSTIC GUITAR
00695640 ....$19.95

AEROSMITH 1973-1979
00695106 ....$22.95

AEROSMITH 1979-1998
00695219 ....$22.95

BEST OF AGGRO-METAL
00695592 ....$19.95

BEST OF CHET ATKINS
00695752 ....$22.95

THE BEACH BOYS DEFINITIVE COLLECTION
00695683 ....$22.95

BEST OF THE BEATLES FOR ACOUSTIC GUITAR
00695453 ....$22.95

THE BEATLES BASS
00695283 ....$22.95

THE BEATLES FAVORITES
00695096 ....$24.95

THE BEATLES HITS
00695049 ....$24.95

BEST OF GEORGE BENSON
00695418 ....$22.95

BEST OF BLACK SABBATH
00695249 ....$22.95

BEST OF BLINK-182
00695704 ....$22.95

BEST OF BLUES GUITAR
00695846 ....$19.95

BLUES GUITAR CLASSICS
00695177 ....$19.95

BLUES/ROCK GUITAR MASTERS
00695348 ....$19.95

KENNY BURRELL
00695830 ....$22.95

BEST OF CHARLIE CHRISTIAN
00695584 ....$22.95

BEST OF ERIC CLAPTON
00695038 ....$24.95

ERIC CLAPTON – THE BLUESMAN
00695040 ....$22.95

ERIC CLAPTON – FROM THE ALBUM UNPLUGGED
00695250 ....$24.95

BEST OF CREAM
00695251 ....$22.95

CREEDANCE CLEARWATER REVIVAL
00695924 ....$22.95

DEEP PURPLE – GREATEST HITS
00695625 ....$22.95

THE BEST OF DEF LEPPARD
00696516 ....$22.95

THE DOORS
00695373 ....$22.95

FAMOUS ROCK GUITAR SOLOS
00695590 ....$19.95

BEST OF FOO FIGHTERS
00695481 ....$22.95

ROBBEN FORD
00695903 ....$22.95

GREATEST GUITAR SOLOS OF ALL TIME
00695301 ....$19.95

BEST OF GRANT GREEN
00695747 ....$22.95

GUITAR INSTRUMENTAL HITS
00695309 ....$19.95

GUITAR RIFFS OF THE '60S
00695218 ....$19.95

BEST OF GUNS N' ROSES
00695183 ....$22.95

HARD ROCK SOLOS
00695591 ....$19.95

JIMI HENDRIX
00696560 ....$24.95

HOT COUNTRY GUITAR
00695580 ....$19.95

BEST OF JAZZ GUITAR
00695586 ....$24.95

ERIC JOHNSON
00699317 ....$24.95

ROBERT JOHNSON
00695264 ....$22.95

THE ESSENTIAL ALBERT KING
00695713 ....$22.95

B.B. KING – THE DEFINITIVE COLLECTION
00695635 ....$22.95

THE KINKS
00695553 ....$22.95

BEST OF KISS
00699413 ....$22.95

MARK KNOPFLER
00695178 ....$22.95

LYNYRD SKYNYRD
00695872 ....$24.95

BEST OF YNGWIE MALMSTEEN
00695669 ....$22.95

BEST OF PAT MARTINO
00695632 ....$22.95

WES MONTGOMERY
00695387 ....$24.95

BEST OF NIRVANA
00695483 ....$24.95

THE OFFSPRING
00695852 ....$24.95

VERY BEST OF OZZY OSBOURNE
00695431 ....$22.95

BEST OF JOE PASS
00695730 ....$22.95

PINK FLOYD – EARLY CLASSICS
00695566 ....$22.95

THE POLICE
00695724 ....$22.95

THE GUITARS OF ELVIS
00696507 ....$22.95

BEST OF QUEEN
00695097 ....$24.95

BEST OF RAGE AGAINST THE MACHINE
00695480 ....$24.95

RED HOT CHILI PEPPERS
00695173 ....$22.95

RED HOT CHILI PEPPERS – GREATEST HITS
00695828 ....$24.95

BEST OF DJANGO REINHARDT
00695660 ....$24.95

BEST OF ROCK
00695884 ....$19.95

BEST OF ROCK 'N' ROLL GUITAR
00695559 ....$19.95

BEST OF ROCKABILLY GUITAR
00695785 ....$19.95

THE ROLLING STONES
00695079 ....$24.95

BEST OF JOE SATRIANI
00695216 ....$22.95

BEST OF SILVERCHAIR
00695488 ....$2

THE BEST OF SOUL GUITAR
00695703 ....$

BEST OF SOUTHERN ROCK
00695560 ....$

ROD STEWART
00695663 ....$2

BEST OF SURF GUITAR
00695822 ....$

BEST OF SYSTEM OF A DOW
00695788 ....$

STEVE VAI
00673247 ....$2

STEVE VAI – ALIEN LOVE SECRETS: THE NAKED VAMP
00695223 ....$

STEVE VAI – FIRE GARDEN: THE NAKED VAMPS
00695166 ....$2

STEVE VAI – THE ULTRA ZON NAKED VAMPS
00695684 ....$2

STEVIE RAY VAUGHAN
00699316 ....$2

THE GUITAR STYLE OF STEVIE RAY VAUGHAN
00695155 ....$2

BEST OF THE VENTURES
00695772 ....$

THE WHO
00695561 ....$

BEST OF ZZ TOP
00695738 ....$2

Complete descriptions and songlists online!

FOR MORE INFORMATION, SEE YOUR LOCAL MUSIC DEALER, OR WRITE TO:

HAL•LEONARD® CORPORATION
7777 W. BLUEMOUND RD. P.O. BOX 13819 MILWAUKEE, WI 53213

www.halleonard.com

Prices, contents and availability subject to change without notice.